ADVANCED ENGLISH READINGS

(With Annotations)

Cho, Suk-chong

신아사

책 머리에

이 책은 대학 영어영문학과의 고급 영문강독, 영어산문, 영미수필 등의 과목의 강독 교재로 꾸몄다.

이러한 목적에 부응하는 책이 영어를 모국어로 사용하는 나라에서는 많이 쏟아져 나오고 있으나 많은 내용이 특정 지역이나 특정 계층의 사람들에게만 흥미를 끌 수 있는 것이거나 아니면 그 나라에 대한 많은 지식이 없이는 이해하기 어려운 것도 있어 그대로 우리나라의 대학 교재로 다루기에는 부적절한 것이 사실이다. 그래서 이러한 과목을 담당하시는 분들은 이 책 저책에서 글을 뽑아 복사하여 가르치기 마련이다.

인문, 사회, 과학 등 여러 분야에 걸쳐 교양인이면 한번쯤은 읽어 볼 가치가 있는 주제들에 대하여 각 분야를 대표할 만한 석학들의 주옥 같은 명문들을 하나의 책에 담아 보았으면 하는 소망을 간직해 왔었다. 그러던 중 93~94년에 영국 Newcastle대학에서 연구하는 동안 여러 책에서 가려 뽑은 자료들과 전부터 모아 둔 자료를 합쳐 간추리기를 거듭하고 주석을 붙이고 읽은 내용을 재음미하는 뜻에서 뒤에 연습문제를 붙여 하나의 책으로 세상에 내 놓는다. 특히 매 과 끝에 실은 다양한 종류의 많은 연습문제는 각 과의 내용을 얼마나 이해하고 있는가를 진단하는 좋은 척도가 될 것이며 이러한 연습문제를 통하여 글을 읽을 때 주의를 기울여야 할 것을 스스로 파악하게 될 것이다. 그와 동시에 가르치는 분들에게는 좋은 평가자료로 활용될 수 있을 것이다.

이 책이 영어 학도는 말할 것도 없고 영어에 관심 있는 현대인에게 영어에 대한 흥미를 더해 주고 사고의 폭을 넓혀 줄 마음의 양식이 되었으면 하는 바램을 조심스럽게 가져 본다.

편자의 무지와 실수로 인한 잘못된 주석이나 오식은 차후 여러분들의 조언에 따라 바로 잡을 것이다. 끝으로 이러한 책이 경제성이 없는데도 쾌히 출판을 허락해 주신 신아사 정현걸 사장님께 고마운 마음을 표하는 바이다.

1995년 가을

편저자

Contents

1. Altruistic Behavior

DESMOND MORRIS*

Altruism[1] is the performance of an unselfish act. As a pattern of behavior this act must have two properties: it must benefit someone else, and it must do so to the disadvantage of the benefactor. It is not merely a matter of being helpful, it is helpfulness at a cost to yourself.

This simple definition conceals a difficult biological problem. If I harm myself to help you, then I am increasing your chances of success relative to mine. In broad evolutionary terms, if I do this, your offspring (or potential offspring) will have better prospects than mine. Because I have been altruistic, your genetic line will stand a better chance of survival than mine. Over a period of time, my unselfish line will die out and your selfish line will survive. So altruism will not be a viable proposition in evolutionary terms.

Since human beings are animals whose ancestors have won the long struggle for survival during their evolutionary history, they cannot be genetically programmed to display true altruism. Evolution theory suggests that they must, like all other animals, be

---

* **Desmond Morris(1928~):** 영국의 인류학자, 작가. 저서로 The Naked Ape, Intimate Behavior등이 있음

1. consideration of the happiness and good of others before one's own (cf. egoism)

entirely selfish in their actions, even when they appear to be at their most self-sacrificing and philanthropic.

This is the biological, evolutionary argument and it is completely convincing as far as it goes, but it does not seem to explain many of mankind's "finer moments." If a man sees a burning house and inside it his small daughter, an old friend, a complete stranger, or even a screaming kitten, he may, without pausing to think, rush headlong into the building and be badly burned in a desperate attempt to save a life. How can actions of this sort be described as selfish? The fact is that they can, but it requires a special definition of the term "self."

When you think of your "self," you probably think of your living body, complete, as it is at this moment. But biologically it is more correct to think of yourself as merely a temporary housing, a disposable container, for your genes. Your genes—the genetic material that you inherited from your parents and which you will pass on to your children—are in a sense immortal. Our bodies are merely the carriers which they use to transport themselves from one generation to the next. It is they, not we, who are the basic units of evolution. We are only their guardians, protecting them from destruction as best we can, for the brief span of our lives.

Religion pictures man as having an immortal soul which leaves his body at death and floats off to heaven (or hell, as the case may be), but the more useful image is to visualize a man's immortal soul as sperm-shaped and a woman's as egg-shaped, and to think of them as leaving the body during the breeding process rather than at death. Following this line of thought through, there is, of course, an afterlife, but it is not in some mysterious "other world," it is right here in the heaven (or hell) of the nursery and the playground, where our genes continue their immortal journey down the tunnel of time, re-housed now in the brand-new flesh-containers we call children.

So, genetically speaking, our children are us—or, rather, half of us, since our mate has a half share of the genes of each child. This makes our devoted and apparently selfless parental care nothing more than *genetic self-care*. The man who risks death to save his small daughter from a fire is in reality saving his own genes in their new body-package. And in saving his genes, his act becomes biologically selfish, rather than altruistic.

But supposing the man leaping into the fire is trying to save, not his daughter, but an old friend? How can this be selfish? The answer here lies in the ancient history of mankind. For more than a million years, man was a simple tribal being, living in small groups where everyone knew everyone else and everyone was closely genetically related to everyone else. Despite a certain amount of outbreeding, the chances were that every member of your own tribe was a relative of some kind, even if a rather remote one. A certain degree of altruism was therefore appropriate where all the other members of your tribe were concerned. You would be helping copies of your own genes, and although you might not respond so intensely to their calls for help as you would do with your own children, you would nevertheless give them a degree of help, again on a basis of genetic selfishness.

This is not, of course, a calculated process. It operates unconsciously and is based on an emotion we call "love." Our love for our children is what we say we are obeying when we act "selflessly" for them, and our love of our fellow-men is what we feel when we come to the aid of our friends. These are inborn tendencies and when we are faced with calls for help we feel ourselves obeying these deep-seated urges unquestioningly and unanalytically. It is only because we see ourselves as "persons" rather than as "gene machines" that we think of these acts of love as unselfish rather than selfish.

So far, so good, but what about the man who rushes headlong into the fire to save a complete stranger? The stranger is probably *not* genetically related to the man who helps him, so this act must surely be truly unselfish and altruistic? The answer is Yes, but only by accident. The accident is caused by the rapid growth of human populations in the last few thousand years. Previously, for millions of years, man was tribal and any inborn urge to help his fellow-men would have meant automatically that he was helping gene-sharing relatives, even if only remote ones. There was no need for this urge to be selective, because there were no strangers around to create problems. But with the urban explosion, man rapidly found himself in huge communities, surrounded by strangers, and with no time for his genetic constitution to alter to fit the startlingly new circumstances. So his altruism inevitably spread to include all his new fellow-citizens, even though many of them may have been genetically quite unrelated to him.

Politicians, exploiting this ancient urge, were easily able to spread the aid-system even further, to a national level called patriotism, so that men would go and die for their country as if it were their ancient tribe or their family.

The man who leaps into the fire to save a small kitten is a special case. To many people, animals are child-substitutes and receive the same care and love as real children. The kitten-saver is explicable as a man who is going to the aid of his symbolic child. This process of symbolizing, of seeing one thing as a metaphorical equivalent of another, is a powerful tendency of the human animal and it accounts for a great deal of the spread of helpfulness across the human environment.

In particular it explains the phenomenon of dying for a cause. This always gives the appearance of the ultimate in altruistic behavior, but a careful examination of the nature of each cause reveals that there is some basic symbolism at work. A nun who gives her life for Christ is already technically a "bride" of Christ and looks upon all people as the "children" of God. Her symbolism has brought the whole of humanity into her "family circle" and her altruism is for her symbolic family, which to her can become as real as other people's natural families.

In this manner it is possible to explain the biological bases for man's seemingly altruistic behavior. This is in no way intended to belittle such activities, but merely to point out that the more usual, alternative explanations are not necessary. For example, it is often stated that man is fundamentally wicked and that his kind acts are largely the result of the teachings of moralists, philosophers and priests; that if he is left to his own devices he will become increasingly savage, violent and cruel. The confidence trick involved here is that if we accept this viewpoint we will attribute all society's good qualities to the brilliant work of these great teachers. The biological truth appears to be rather different. Since selfishness is genetic rather than personal, we will have a natural tendency to help our blood-relatives and hence our whole tribe. Since our tribes have swollen into nations, our helpfulness becomes stretched further and further, aided and abetted by our tendency toward accepting symbolic substitutes for the real thing. Altogether this means that we are now, by nature, a remarkably helpful species. If there are breakdowns in this helpfulness, they are probably due, not to our "savage nature" reasserting itself, but to the unbearable tensions under which people so often find themselves in the strained and over-crowded world of today.

It would be a mistake, nevertheless, to overstate man's angelic helpfulness. He is also intensely competitive. But under normal circumstances these rival tendencies balance each other out, and this balance accounts for a great deal of human intercourse, in the form of *transactional behavior*. This is behavior of the "I'll-scratch-your-back-if-you'll-scratch-mine" type. We do deals with one another. My actions help you, but they are not altruistic because they also help me at the same time. This co-operative behavior is perhaps the dominant feature of day-to-day social interaction. It is the basis of trade and commerce and it explains why such activities do not become more ruthless. If the competitive element were not tempered by the basic urge to help one another, business practices would rapidly become much more savage and brutal than they are, even today.

An important extension of this two-way co-operative behavior is embodied in the phrase: "one good turn now deserves another later.[2]" This is delayed, or nonspecific co-operation. I give help to you now, even though you cannot help me in return. I do this daily to many people I meet. One day I will need help and then, as part of a "long-term deal," they will return my help. I do not keep a check on what I am owed or by whom. Indeed, the person who finally helps me may not be one of the ones I have helped. But a whole network of social debts will have built up in a community and, as there is a great division of labor and skills in our species today, such a system will be beneficial to all the members of the society. This has been called "reciprocal altruism." But once again it is not true altruism because sooner or later, one way or

---

2. 좋은 일을 해 주면 좋은 일을 받게 마련

another, I will be rewarded for my acts of helpfulness.

Anticipation of a delayed-reward of this kind is often the hidden motive for a great deal of what is claimed to be purely altruistic behavior. Many countries hand out official awards to their citizens for "services to the community," but frequently these services have been deliberately undertaken in the anticipation that they are award-worthy. Comparatively few public honors ever come as a surprise. And many other "good works" are undertaken with later social (or heavenly) rewards in mind. This does not necessarily make the "works" any less good, of course, it merely explains the motives involved.

The following table sums up the relationship between competitiveness and helpfulness, and their intermediates:

1	Self-assertive behavior	Helps me	Harms you	Mild competitiveness to full criminality
2	Self-indulgent behavior	Helps me	No effect on you	The private, non-social pleasures
3	Co-operative behavior	Helps me	Helps you	Transaction, trade, barter, and negotiation
4	Courteous behavior	No effect on me	Helps you	Kindness and generosity
5	"Altruistic" behavior	Harms me	Helps you	Loving devotion, philanthropy, self-sacrifice, and patriotism

EXERCISES

A. *Answer the following questions.*

1. The author defines 'altruism,' 'self,' and 'immortal soul.' What is the method of these definitions? What is their importance?
2. What are two properties of an unselfish act?
3. How does the writer distinguish selfish act from altruistic act?
4. What is meant by genetic selfishness?
5. How does he define true altruism?

B. *Rewrite the following by giving the correct antonyms of certain words so that the statements may be true to the essay.*

1. Altruism is the performance of an unselfish act. As a pattern of behavior this act must have two properties: it must benefit someone else, and it must do so to the advantage of the benefactor.
2. If I harm myself to help you, then I am decreasing your chances of success relative to mine.
3. In broad evolutionary terms, if I do this, your ancestors will have better prospects than mine.
4. Because I have been selfish, your genetic line will stand a better chance of survival than mine.
5. Biologically it is more correct to think of yourself as merely a permanent housing, a disposable container, for your genes.
6. Religion pictures man as having an mortal soul which leaves his body at death and floats off to heaven (or hell, as the case may be).

7. Despite a certain amount of outbreeding, the chances were that every member of your own tribe was a relative of some kind, even if a rather close one.
8. But with the rural explosion, man rapidly found himself in huge communities, surrounded by strangers, and with no time for his genetic constitution to alter to fit the startlingly new circumstances.
9. So his altruism inevitably spread to exclude all his new fellow-citizens, even though many of them may have been genetically quite unrelated to him.
10. It would be a mistake, nevertheless, to understate man's angelic helpfulness.

C. *Fill in the blanks with suitable words.*

1. Our bodies are merely the carriers which they use to transport themselves from one generation to the (   ).
2. So, genetically speaking, our children are us—or, rather, (   ) of us, since our mate has a half share of the genes of each child.
3. And in saving his genes, his act becomes biologically (   ), rather than altruistic.
4. It is only because we see ourselves as "persons" rather than as "gene machines" (   ) we think of these acts of love as unselfish rather than selfish.
5. Altogether this means that we are now, (   ) nature, a remarkably helpful species.

2. How to Read Body Language

DAVID ABERCROMBIE*

All of us communicate with one another nonverbally, as well as with words. Most of the time we're not aware that we're doing it. We gesture with eyebrows or a hand, meet someone else's eyes and look away, shift positions in a chair. These actions we assume are random and incidental. But researchers have discovered in recent years that there is a system to them almost as consistent and comprehensible as language.

Every culture has its own body language, and children absorb its nuances along with spoken language. A Frenchman talks and moves in French. The way an Englishman crosses his legs is nothing like the way a male American does it. In talking, Americans are apt to end a statement with a droop of the head or hand, a lowering of the eyelids. They wind up a question with a lift of the hand, a tilt of the chin or a widening of the eyes. With a future-tense verb they often gesture with a forward movement.

There are regional idioms too: an expert can sometimes pick out a native of Wisconsin just by the way he uses his eyebrows during conversation. Your sex, ethnic background, social class

---

* **David Abercrombie(1909～):** Scotland의 Edinburgh대학 음성학 교수, English Phonetic Texts (1964)등의 저서가 있음

and personal style all influence your body language. Nevertheless, you move and gesture within the American idiom. The person who is truly bilingual is also bilingual in body language. New York's famous mayor, Fiorello La Guardia, politicked in English, Italian and Yiddish. When films of his speeches are run without sound, it's not too difficult to identify from his gestures the language he was speaking. One of the reasons English-dubbed foreign films often seem flat is that the gestures don't match the language.

Usually, the wordless communication acts to qualify the words. What the nonverbal elements express very often, and very efficiently, is the emotional side of the message. When a person feels liked or disliked, often it's a case of "not what he said but the way he said it." Psychologist Albert Mehrabian has devised this formula: total impact of a message = 7 percent verbal + 38 percent vocal + 55 percent facial. The importance of the voice can be seen when you consider that even the words "I hate you" can be made to sound sexy.

Experts in kinesics—the study of communication through body movement—are not prepared to spell out[1] a precise vocabulary of gestures. When an American rubs his nose, it may mean he is disagreeing with someone or rejecting something. But there are other possible interpretations, too. Another example: when a student in conversation with a professor holds the older man's eyes a little longer than is usual, it can be a sign of respect and affection; it can be a subtle challenge to the professor's authority; or it can be something else entirely. The expert looks for patterns in the context, not for an isolated meaningful gesture.

---

1. 철자를 쓰듯이 명확하게 설명하다

Kinesics is a young science and very much the brainchild of one man, anthropologist Dr. Ray L. Birdwhistell. But it already offers a wide variety of small observations. (For example: eyebrows have a repertoire of about 23 possible positions; men use their eyebrows more than women do.) Most people find they can shut out conversation[2] and concentrate on watching body language for only about 30 seconds at a time. Anyone can experiment with it, however, simply by turning on the television picture without the sound. One of the most potent elements in body language is eye behavior. Americans are careful about how and when they meet one another's eyes. In our normal conversation, each eye contact lasts only about a second before one or both individuals look away. When two Americans look searchingly into each other's eyes, emotions are heightened and the relationship becomes more intimate. Therefore, we carefully avoid this, except in appropriate circumstances.

Americans abroad sometimes find local eye behavior hard to interpret. "Tel Aviv was disturbing," one man recalled. "People stared right at me on the street; they looked me up and down. I kept wondering if I was uncombed or unzipped. Finally, a friend explained that Israelis think nothing of staring at others on the street."

Proper street behavior in the United States requires a nice balance of attention and inattention. You are supposed to look at a passerby just enough to show that you're aware of his presence. If you look too little, you appear haughty or secretive; too much, and you're inquisitive. Usually what happens is that people eye each other until they are about eight feet apart, at which point both cast down their eyes. Sociologist Dr. Erving Goffman describes this as

---

2. 대화에 귀기울이지 않다

"a kind of dimming of lights[3]." In parts of the Far East it is impolite to look at the other person at all during conversation. In England the polite listener stares at the speaker attentively and blinks his eyes occasionally as a sign of interest. That eye-blink says nothing to Americans, who expect the listener to nod or to murmur something—such as "mm-hmm."

There are times when what a person says with his body gives the lie to what he is saying with his tongue. Sigmund Freud once wrote: "No mortal can keep a secret. If his lips are silent, he chatters with his fingertips; betrayal oozes out of him at every pore."

Thus, a man may successfully control his face, and appear calm, self-controlled—unaware that signs of tension and anxiety are leaking out, that his foot is beating the floor constantly, restlessly, as if it had a life of its own. Rage is another emotion feet and legs may reveal. During arguments the feet often become tense. Fear sometimes produces barely perceptible running motions, a kind of nervous leg jiggle. Then there are the subtle, provocative leg gestures that women use, consciously and unconsciously.

Recent studies by psychologists suggest that posture often reflects a person's attitude toward people he is with. One experiment indicates that when men are with other men they dislike, they relax either very little or very much—depending on whether they see the other man as threatening. Women in this experiment always signaled dislike with very relaxed posture. And men, paired with women they disliked, were never tense enough about it to sit rigidly.

Postures sometimes offer a guide to broad relationships within

---

3. 본래 마주 오는 차를 위해 자동차 불빛을 아래로 향한다는 뜻에서 상대를 바로 보지 않고 시선을 낮춘다는 뜻

a group. Imagine that at a party, guests have been fired up by an argument over student radicalism. You may be able to spot at a glance the two sides of the argument by postures adopted. Most of the pros, for example, may sit with crossed knees, the cons with legs stretched out and arms folded. A few middle-of-the-roaders may try a little of each—crossing their knees *and* folding their arms. If an individual abruptly shifts his body around in his chair, it may mean that he disagrees with the speaker or even that he is changing sides.[4] None of this, of course, represents an infallible guide, but it is apparently significant enough to be worth watching for.

While children learn spoken and body language—proper postures, eye behaviors, etc.—they also learn a subtler thing: how to react to space around them. Man walks around inside a kind of private bubble, which represents the amount of air space he feels he must have between himself and other people. Anthropologists, working with cameras, have recorded the tremors and minute eye movements that betray the moment the individual's bubble is breached. As adults, however, we hide our feelings behind a screen of polite words.

Anthropologist Dr. Edward T. Hall points out that, for two unacquainted adult male North Americans, the comfortable distance to stand for private conversation is from arm's length to about four feet apart. The South American likes to stand much closer, which creates problems when the two meet face to face. For, as the South American moves in, the North American feels he's being pushy;[5] and as the North American backs off, the South American thinks he's being standoffish.

The American and the Arab are even less compatible in their

---

4. 딴 편으로 옮아 가다
5. unpleasantly aggressive

space habits. Arabs like close contact. In some instances, they stand very close together to talk, staring intently into each other's eyes and breathing into each other's face. These are actions the American may associate with sexual intimacy and he may find it disturbing to be subjected to them in a nonsexual context.

The amount of space a man needs is also influenced by his personality—introvert, for example, seem to need more elbow room than extroverts. Situation and mood also affect distance. Moviegoers waiting in line to see a sexy film will line up much more densely than those waiting to see a family-entertainment movie.

George du Maurier once wrote: "Language is a poor thing. You fill your lungs with wind and shake a little slit in your throat and make mouths[6] , and that shakes the air; and the air shakes a pair of little drums in my head .... and my brain seizes your meaning in the rough.[7] What a roundabout way and what a waste of time!"[8]

Communication between human beings would be just that dull if it were all done with words. But actually, words are often the smallest part of it.

---

6. 입의 모양을 취하다
7. 대충
8. 다음에 our verbal language is 가 생략되어 있음

EXERCISES

A. *Answer the following questions.*

1. What is the main idea of this article?
2. What does 'chatter with one's fingertips' mean?
3. What differences have you noticed in gestures, facial expression, keeping distance, embracing, shaking hands, or eye behavior in the foreigners?
4. Do you feel that Dr. Birdwhistell's theory is valid?
5. Do you think that a science of kinesics really exists?

B. *Rewrite each sentence, choosing an appropriate synonym from the list below for the italicized words. Be sure to use the correct forms.*

a. powerful	b. very tense
c. moderate	d. very delicate shades of meaning
e. arrogant	f. to suppose
g. anger	h. curious
i. very small	j. to agree with

1. Children are usually *inquisitive* about things around them.
2. Do not take too much of this medicine because it's very *potent*.
3. The calculus professor *assumed* that we had already mastered basic geometry and algebra.
4. Your report of the incident *is consistent with* his report.
5. Unfortunately, he became rather *haughty* after he won the election.

6. That story is not easy to comprehend because it is full of *nuance*.
7. You should try to keep your *rage* under control.
8. Many students feel *nervous* before examinations.
9. Most Americans are *middle-of-the-roaders*, according to that survey.
10. A perfectionist is often concerned with *minute* details.

C. *Write "T" after true statements and "F" after false statements.*

1. According to this article, facial expression and body movements are as important as words in communication.
2. The person most responsible for kinesics — the study of communication through body movement — was Sigmund Freud.
3. Men use their eyebrows more than women do.
4. In a normal conversation between Americans, eye contact lasts about 4 seconds before one or both individuals look away.
5. According to this article, in certain parts of the Far East, people watch each other attentively during a polite conversation.
6. Americans and Englishmen act differently when they are listening attentively.
7. When a woman is with someone she does not like, she always assumes a very relaxed posture.
8. When a man is with a man he does not like, he sometimes assumes a very relaxed posture.
9. South Americans and Arabs are more similar in their space requirements than North Americans and Arabs are.
10. A very aggressive, outgoing person needs less space than a passive, introverted person.

3. Work and Play

HERBERT READ*

What do we mean by leisure, and why should we assume that it represents a problem to be solved by the arts? The great ages of art were not conspicuous for their leisure—at least, art was not an activity associated with leisure. It was a craft like any other, concerned with the making of necessary things. Leisure, in the present meaning of the word, did not exist. Leisure, before the Industrial Revolution, meant no more than 'time' or 'opportunity'; 'If your leisure served, I would speak with you',[1] says one of Shakespeare's characters. Phrases which we still use, such as 'at your leisure', preserve this original meaning.

But when we speak of leisure nowadays, we are not thinking of securing time or opportunity to do something; time is heavy on our hands,[2] and the problem is how to fill it. Leisure no longer signifies a space with some difficulty secured against the pressure of events: rather it is a pervasive emptiness for which we must invent occupations. Leisure is a vacuum, a desperate state of vacancy—a vacancy of mind and body. It has been commandeered by the sociologists and the psychologists: it is a problem.

Our diurnal existence is divided into two phases, as distinct as

---

* **Herbert Read(1893～1968):** 영국의 시인, 미술 및 사회 비평가

1. If you had sufficient time, ... (*Much Ado about Nothing*에서 Don John 이 한 말)

2. we have plenty of time and do not know what to do with it

day and night. We call them *work* and *play*. We work so many hours a day, and, when we have allowed the necessary minimum for such activities as eating and shopping, the rest we spend in various activities which are known as *recreations*, an elegant word which disguises the fact that we usually do not even play in our hours of leisure, but spend them in various forms of passive enjoyment or entertainment—not football but watching football matches; not acting, but theater-going; not walking, but riding in a motor coach.

We need to make, therefore, a hard-and-fast distinction not only between work and play but, equally, between active play and passive entertainment. It is, I suppose, the decline of active play—of amateur sport—and the enormous growth of purely receptive entertainment which has given rise to a sociological interest in the problem. If the greater part of the population, instead of indulging in sport, spend their hours of leisure 'viewing' television programmes, there will inevitably be a decline in health and physique. And, in addition, there will be a psychological problem, for we have yet to trace the mental and moral consequences of a prolonged diet of sentimental or sensational spectacles on the screen. There is, if we are optimistic, the possibility that the diet is too thin and unnourishing to have much permanent effect on anybody. Nine films out of ten seem to leave absolutely no impression on the mind or imagination of those who see them: few people can give a coherent account of the film they saw the week before last, and at longer intervals they must rely on the management to see that they do not sit through the same film twice.

We have to live art if we would be affected by art. We have to paint rather than look at paintings, to play instruments rather than go to concerts, to dance and sing and act ourselves, engaging all our senses in the ritual and discipline of the arts. Then something may begin to happen to us: to work upon our bodies and our souls.

It is only when entertainment is active, participated in, practised, that it can properly be called play, and as such it is a natural use of leisure. In that sense play stands in contrast to work, and is usually regarded as an activity that alternates with work. It is there that the final and most fundamental error enters into our conception of daily life.

Work itself is not a single concept. We say quite generally that we work in order to make a living: to earn, that is to say, sufficient tokens which we can exchange for food and shelter and all the other needs of our existence. But some of us work physically, tilling the land, minding the machines, digging the coal; others work mentally, keeping accounts, inventing machines, teaching and preaching, managing and governing. There does not seem to be any factor common to all these diverse occupations, except that they consume our time, and leave us little leisure.

We may next observe that one man's profession or work is often another man's recreation or play. The merchant at the week-end becomes a hunter (he has not yet taken to mining); the clerk becomes a gardener; the machine-tender becomes a breeder of bull-terriers. There is, of course, a sound instinct behind such transformations. The body and mind are unconsciously seeking compensation—muscular coordination, mental integration. But in many cases a dissociation is set up and the individual leads a double life—one half Jekyll, the other half Hyde.[3] There is a profound moral behind that story of Stevenson's, for the compensation which a disintegrated personality may seek will often be of an anti-social nature. The Nazi party, for example, in its early days was largely recruited from the bored—not so much

3. 진지하고 선량한 의사가 자기 자신으로 그리고 비인간적인 괴물인 Mr. Hyde로 이중성격을 가지고 있는

from the unemployed as from the street-corner society of listless hooligans.

Scientific studies have been made of street-corner society,[4] out of which crime, gangsterdom, and fascism inevitably develop. It is a society with leisure—that is to say, spare time—and without compensatory occupation. It does not need a Satan to find mischief for such idle hands to do. They will spontaneously itch to do something: muscles have a life of their own unless they are trained to purposeful actions. Actions, or rather activities, are the obvious reflex to leisure; they consume it, and leave the problem solved.

But work is also activity, and if we reach the conclusion that all our time must be filled with one activity or another, the distinction between work and play becomes rather meaningless, and what we mean by play is merely a change of occupation. We pass from one form of activity to another; one we call work, and for that we receive pay; the other we call play, and for that we receive no pay—on the contrary, we probably pay a subscription.

The six most important words are: I admit I made a mistake.
The five most important words are: You did a good job.
The four most important words are: What is your opinion?
The three most important words are: If you please.
The two most important words are: Thank you.
The least important word is: I.

4. 한가하게 거리 모퉁이에 모이는 온갖 집단의 사람들

EXERCISES

A. *Answer the following questions.*

1. What is the present meaning of leisure?
2. What is meant by passive enjoyment or entertainment?
3. What is meant by "to live art"?
4. What can we properly call play?
5. How can you distinguish work from play?
6. How has the Industrial Revolution changed the nature of both our professional activities (work) and our hobbies (play)?

B. *Read the following statements based on the essay. Write T if a statement is true, and F if it is false.*

1. Many people nowadays think that leisure is a problem which should be solved by the arts.
2. Before the Industrial Revolution, the word 'leisure' did not exist.
3. 'The great ages of art' which the author mentions came after the Industrial Revolution.
4. Shakespeare used the word 'leisure' to mean 'time' or 'opportunity'.
5. Nowadays sociologists and psychologists have made leisure a problem.
6. In the past, leisure 'signified a space with some difficulty secured against the pressure of events'.
7. The words 'work' and 'play' are generally used to refer to day and night.
8. Activities such as eating and shopping are generally included

in 'play'.

9. We need to make a distinction not between work and play but between active play and passive entertainment.
10. If people spent their leisure in active play, there would probably be no sociological problem about leisure.
11. A majority of the films we see are full of sentiment and exciting scenes.
12. The author is sorry that people cannot remember the films they have seen, even for a couple of weeks.
13. Activities such as painting, dancing and singing should not be regarded as 'play'.
14. It is a 'fundamental error' to think that 'play stands in contrast to work'.
15. Two things are common to all kinds of 'work': they consume our time and they bring us money.
16. Merchants will never take to mining at the week-end.
17. The author's examples of 'work' and 'play' show a natural connection between the two: those who do mental 'work' like to get physical exercise in 'play'; those who 'work' with machines like to 'play' with animals.
18. Whenever 'play' is different from 'work', a dissociation is set up and the individual leads a double life.
19. When work and play are not properly coördinated, they become unconnected activities and the individual begins to lead a double life.
20. 'A disintegrated personality' here means a person who leads a double life.
21. A disintegrated personality always seeks anti-social work.
22. The Nazi party, in its early days,consisted entirely of unemployed persons.

23. The absence of 'play' leads to boredom and restlessness, which often lead to anti-social work.
24. Muscles have a life of their own only in street-corner societies.
25. All purposeful actions or activities should be regarded as 'work', according to the author.

C. *Write down three forms for each of the following words, and mark the stress for each form. Refer to a dictionary.*

1. 'signify *sig'nificant* *signifi'cation*
2. character
3. compensate
4. destroy
5. equal

D. *Find single words or phrases in the passage which have roughly the meanings given below.*

1. done for pleasure and not for money
2. anything of small value which can be exchanged for goods of much higher value
3. clear; well-arranged
4. all the set forms connected with a performance or ceremony
5. influenced
6. response (in which the will or mind plays no part)

4. How to Mark a Book

MORTIMER J. ADLER*

You know you have to read "between the lines"[1] to get the most out of anything. I want to persuade you to do something equally important in the course of your reading. I want to persuade you to "write between the lines." Unless you do, you are not likely to do the most efficient kind of reading.

I contend, quite bluntly, that marking up a book is not an act of mutilation but of love.

You shouldn't mark up a book which isn't yours. Librarians (or your friends) who lend you books expect you to keep them clean, and you should. If you decide that I am right about the usefulness of marking books, you will have to buy them. Most of the world's great books are available today, in reprint editions, at less than a dollar.

There are two ways in which one can own a book. The first is the property right you establish by paying for it, just as you pay for clothes and furniture. But this act of purchase is only the prelude to possession. Full ownership comes only when you have made it a part of yourself, and the best way to make yourself a part of it is by writing in it. An illustration may make the point clear. You

---

*** Mortimer J. Adler(1902～):** 미국의 철학자, 교육자

1. 언외의 숨은 뜻을 알아내다

buy a beefsteak and transfer it from the butcher's icebox to your own. But you do not own the beefsteak in the most important sense until you consume it and get it into your bloodstream. I am arguing that books, too, must be absorbed in your bloodstream to do you any good.

Confusion about what it means to own a book leads people to a false reverence for paper, binding, and type—a respect for the physical thing—the craft of the printer rather than the genius of the author. They forget that it is possible for a man to acquire the idea, to possess the beauty, which a great book contains, without staking his claim[2] by pasting his bookplate inside the cover. Having a fine library doesn't prove that its owner has a mind enriched by books; it proves nothing more than that he, his father, or his wife, was rich enough to buy them.

There are three kinds of book owners. The first has all the standard sets and best-sellers—unread, untouched. (This deluded individual owns woodpulp and ink, not books.) The second has a great many books—a few of them read through, most of them dipped into[3], but all of them as clean and shiny as the day they were bought. (This person would probably like to make books his own, but is restrained by a false respect for their physical appearance.) The third has a few books or many—every one of them dog-eared and dilapidated, shaken and loosened by continual use, marked and scribbled in from front to back. (This man owns books.)

Is it false respect, you may ask, to preserve intact and unblemished a beautifully printed book, an elegantly bound

---

2. make a claim, 가질 권리가 있다고 말하다
3. 별다른 주의를 기울이지 않고 잠시 읽다

edition? Of course not. I'd no more scribble all over a first edition of "Paradise Lost" than I'd give my baby a set of crayons and an original Rembrandt! I wouldn't mark up a painting or a statue. Its soul, so to speak, is inseparable from its body. And the beauty of a rare edition or of a richly manufactured volume is like that of a painting or a statue.

But the soul of a book *can* be separated from its body. A book is more like the score of a piece of music than it is like a painting. No great musician confuses a symphony with the printed sheets of music. Arturo Toscanini[4] reveres Brahms, but Toscanini's score of the C-minor Symphony is so thoroughly marked up that no one but the maestro himself can read it. The reason why a great conductor makes notations on his musical scores—marks them up again and again each time he returns to study them—is the reason why you should mark your books. If your respect for magnificent binding or typography gets in the way[5], buy yourself a cheap edition and pay your respects to the author.

Why is marking up a book indispensable to reading? First, it keeps you awake. (And I don't mean merely conscious; I mean wide awake.) In the second place, reading, if it is active, is thinking, and thinking tends to express itself in words, spoken or written. The marked book is usually the thought-through book. Finally, writing helps you remember the thoughts you had, or the thoughts the author expressed. Let me develop these three points.

If reading is to accomplish anything more than passing time, it must be active. You can't let your eyes glide across the lines of a

4. Arturo Toscanini(1867～1957): Italy태생의 미국 관현악 지휘자
5. 방해가 되다

book and come up with[6] an understanding of what you have read. Now an ordinary piece of light fiction, like, say, "Gone with the Wind," doesn't require the most active kind of reading. The books you read for pleasure can be read in a state of relaxation, and nothing is lost. But a great book, rich in ideas and beauty, a book that raises and tries to answer great fundamental questions, demands the most active reading of which you are capable. You don't absorb the ideas of John Dewey the way you absorb the crooning of Mr. Vallee. You have to reach for them. That you cannot do while you're asleep.

If, when you've finished reading a book, the pages are filled with your notes, you know that you read actively. The most famous *active* reader of great books I know is President Hutchins of the University of Chicago. He also has the hardest schedule of business activities of any man I know. He invariably reads with a pencil, and sometimes, when he picks up a book and pencil in the evening, he finds himself, instead of making intelligent notes, drawing what he calls "caviar factories"[7] on the margins. When that happens, he puts the book down. He knows he's too tired to read, and he's just wasting time.

But, you may ask, why is writing necessary? Well, the physical act of writing, with your own hand, brings words and sentences more sharply before your mind and preserves them better in your memory. To set down[8] your reaction to important words and sentences you have read, and the questions they have raised in your mind, is to preserve those reactions and sharpen

---

6. think of a plan; produce
7. 철갑상어등의 알을 절인 것을 caviar라 하는데 여기서는 뭔가를 생각하면서 하는 낙서, doodling
8. to make a written record of

those questions.

Even if you wrote on a scratch pad[9], and threw the paper away when you had finished writing, your grasp of the book would be surer. But you don't have to throw the paper away. The margins (top and bottom, as well as side), the end-papers, the very space between the lines, are all available. They aren't sacred. And, best of all, your marks and notes become an integral part of the book and stay there forever. You can pick up the book the following week or year, and there are all your points of agreement, disagreement, doubt, and inquiry. It's like resuming an interrupted conversation with the advantage of being able to pick up where you left off.

And that is exactly what reading a book should be: a conversation between you and the author. Presumably he knows more about the subject than you do; naturally, you'll have the proper humility as you approach him. But don't let anybody tell you that a reader is supposed to be solely on the receiving end. Understanding is a two-way operation; learning doesn't consist in being an empty receptacle. The learner has to question himself and question the teacher. He even has to argue with the teacher, once he understands what the teacher is saying. And marking a book is literally an expression of your differences, or agreements of opinion, with the author.

There are all kinds of devices for marking a book intelligently and fruitfully. Here's the way I do it:

1. *Underlining:* of major points, of important or forceful statements.

---

9. 잡기용지철

2. *Vertical lines at the margin:* to emphasize a statement already underlined.
3. *Star, asterisk, or other doo-dad*[10] *at the margin:* to be used sparingly, to emphasize the ten or twenty most important statements in the book. (You may want to fold the bottom corner of each page on which you use such marks. It won't hurt the sturdy paper on which most modern books are printed, and you will be able to take the book off the shelf at any time and, by opening it at the folded-corner page, refresh your recollection of the book.)
4. *Numbers in the margin:* to indicate the sequence of points the author makes in developing a single argument.
5. *Numbers of other pages in the margin:* to indicate where else in the book the author made points relevant to the point marked; to tie up the ideas in a book, which, though they may be separated by many pages, belong together.
6. *Circling of key words or phrases.*
7. *Writing in the margin, or at the top or bottom of the page, for the sake of :* recording questions (and perhaps answers) which a passage raised in your mind; reducing a complicated discussion to a simple statement; recording the sequence of major points right through the book. I use the end-papers at the back of the book to make a personal index of the author's points in the order of their appearance.

The front end-papers are, to me, the most important. Some people reserve them for a fancy bookplate. I reserve them for fancy thinking. After I have finished reading the book and making

10. 이름이 생각나지 않는 것의 대용어, 즉 거시기

my personal index on the back end-papers, I turn to the front and try to outline the book, not page by page, or point by point (I've already done that at the back), but as an integrated structure, with a basic unity and an order of parts. This outline is, to me, the measure of my understanding of the work.

If you're a die-hard anti-book marker, you may object that the margins, the space between the lines, and the end-papers don't give you room enough. All right. How about using a scratch pad slightly smaller than the pagesize of the book—so that the edges of the sheets won't protrude? Make your index, outlines, and even your notes on the pad, and then insert these sheets permanently inside the front and back covers of the book.

Or, you may say that this business of marking books is going to slow up your reading. It probably will. That's one of the reasons for doing it. Most of us have been taken in[11] by the notion that speed of reading is a measure of our intelligence. There is no such thing as the right speed for intelligent reading. Some things should be read quickly and effortlessly, and some should be read slowly and even laboriously. The sign of intelligence in reading is the ability to read different things differently according to their worth. In the case of good books, the point is not to see how many of them you can get through[12] , but rather how many can get through you—how many you can make your own. A few friends are better than a thousand acquaintances. If this be your aim, as it should be, you will not be impatient if it takes more time and effort to read a great book than it does a newspaper.

---

11. to deceive
12. pass through

You may have one final objection to marking books. You can't lend them to your friends because nobody else can read them without being distracted by your notes. Furthermore, you won't want to lend them because a marked copy is a kind of intellectual diary, and lending it is almost like giving your mind away.

If your friend wishes to read your "Plutarch's Lives," "Shakespeare," or "The Federalist Papers," tell him, gently but firmly, to buy a copy. You will lend him your car or your coat— but your books are as much a part of you as your head or your heart.

EXERCISES

A. *Answer the following questions.*

1. What is meant by active reading?
2. What is meant by writing between the lines?
3. What are two ways in which one can own a book?
4. What are three kinds of book owners?
5. Why does the writer say marking up a book is indispensable to reading?
6. What does the writer say of the speed of reading?

B. *Write in each blank space a word that fits naturally.*

1. I contend that marking up a book is not an act of mutilation (   ) of love.
2. I am arguing that books, too, must be absorbed in your bloodstream to do you any (   ).
3. The second has a great many books — a few of them read through, most of them dipped (   ), but all of them as clean and shiny as the day they were bought.

4. If reading (   ) to accomplish anything more than passing time, it must be active.
5. You can't let your eyes glide across the lines of a book and come up (   ) an understanding of what you have read.
6. You don't absorb the ideas of John Dewey the (   ) you absorb the crooning of Mr. Vallee.
7. But the soul of a book can be separated from its body. A book is more like the score of a piece of music (   ) it is like a painting.
8. If your respect for magnificent binding or typography (   ) in the way, buy yourself a cheap edition.
9. A great book demands the most active reading (   ) which you are capable.
10. To set (   ) your reaction to important words and sentences you have read is to preserve those reactions.
11. It's like resuming an interrupted conversation with the advantage of being able to pick up where you left (   ).
12. You will lend him your car or your coat—but your books are as (   ) a part of you as your head or your heart.

C. *Write in each blank a suitable word that has one of the following meanings.*

a. not spoiled
b. too important or too useful to be without
c. a piece of music for an orchestra
d. a decòrative piece of paper stuck in a book to show who owns it
e. a person whom one knows, but who is not a close friend
f. something which is owned; possessions
g. necessary; which cannot be left out
h. rest and amusement

i. impossible to separate from something else or from one another

j. a planned list or order of things to be done or dealt with

1. The first is the ( ) right you establish by paying for it, just as you pay for clothes and furniture.
2. Is it false respect to preserve intact and ( ) a beautifully printed book, and elegantly bound edition?
3. I wouldn't mark up a painting or a statue. Its soul, so to speak, is ( ) from its body.
4. Why is marking up a book ( ) to reading? First, it keeps you awake.
5. The books you read for pleasure can be read in a state of ( ), and nothing is lost.
6. He also has the hardest ( ) of business activities of any man I know.
7. Your marks and notes become an ( ) part of the book and stay there forever.
8. It is possible for a man to acquire the idea which a great book contains without staking his claim by pasting his ( ) inside the cover.
9. A few friends are better than a thousand ( ).
10. No great musician confuses a ( ) with the printed sheets of music.

D. *Read the following statements carefully and say whether it is true or false, according to the passage you have read.*

1. We are not likely to do the most efficient kind of reading if we don't write between the lines.
2. The author suggests that marking up a book is an act of mutilation.
3. It can be said that you own a book only when you have made

the book a part of yourself.

4. We should pay a respect for the physical appearance of a book as well as the genius of the author.
5. Having a fine library always means that its owner has a mind enriched by books.
6. Writing in the book helps us remember the thoughts we had, or the thoughts the author expressed.
7. An ordinary piece of light fiction requires the most active kind of reading.
8. The physical act of writing brings words and sentences more sharply before our mind and preserves them better in our memory.
9. Understanding is a one-way operation; learning consists in being an empty receptacle.
10. Besides questioning the teacher, the learner has to argue with the teacher, once he understands what the teacher is saying.
11. Most of us do not agree to the notion that speed of reading is a measure of our intelligence.

If anybody would make me the greatest king that ever lived, with palaces, and gardens, and fine dinners, and wine, and coaches, and beautiful clothes, and hundreds of servants, on condition that I would not read books, I would not be a king.

Thomas B. Macaulay

5. Why We Must Control Population Growth

ISAAC ASIMOV*

There are many people who are educated and who know about the world population and the way it is growing but think there is no danger. They tell themselves that people who talk of the danger are foolish and wrong.

People who don't believe there is a crisis can point to the Netherlands, for instance. They say that the Netherlands is prosperous and yet is much more densely populated than the world average. They say that it would do no harm to let the whole world become that densely populated. They don't seem to realize that the Netherlands is prosperous because it has fertile soil and much water; that it makes use of a great deal of industrial products like fertilizer and insecticides; that it imports a great deal of oil and that it has no forests to speak of.

There just isn't enough fertile soil and enough water to make the entire world into one gigantic Netherlands. There isn't enough fertilizer and insecticides and oil, and we don't really want to cut down all the forests. Besides, it won't take very long for the earth

---

* **Isaac Asimov(1920～　　):** 소련 태생의 미국 작가, Boston대학 생화학 교수, The Stars, Like the Dust등 200여권의 저서가 있음

to be as densely populated all over as the Netherlands is now, and if it could be done, how would we stop the population increase at that point?

Some people think that science will solve all problems. They say that more people will just mean more scientists working on those problems. They don't realize that the problems get worse and worse, faster and faster, and that sooner or later—probably sooner—science just won't be able to keep up the pace.

Some people even think that population means strength. They think that large nations with many people can conquer neighboring nations with fewer people. They think that if their own nation does not increase its population, a neighboring nation which *does* increase its population will conquer them. For this reason, some nations think that they must have more and more babies, more and more people, if they are to remain strong and free.

Even if war is not involved, some people think a nation with a large population can keep its own customs, languages, and attitudes better than a nation with a small population. If a neighboring nation grows faster, they think, that neighboring nation might impose *its* customs, language, and attitudes on the smaller one, just by outnumbering them.

Actually, this is not so. Very often in history, small nations have conquered large ones. It's not so much the size of the army as its organization and the technical level of its weapons. Thus, Greece took over[1] Persia in the 300s B.C., Mongolia took over China in the 1200s, and Great Britain took over India in the 1700s, even though Persia, China, and India were far more populous than Greece, Mongolia, and Great Britain.

---

1. 떠맡다, 물려받다

Then, too, the Greek language and culture in ancient times and the English language and culture in modern times spread over the world even though those languages were spoken by few people to begin with.

If a nation wishes to avoid being dominated by its neighbors, its best chance is to raise its standard of living and its level of technology. This can be done best by not allowing its population to grow to such a point that it is sunk in misery and poverty. In fact, the worst way in which a nation can try to avoid being dominated by its neighbor is to increase its population to the point of misery and poverty.

If every nation tries to compete with its neighbors by raising its population, then the whole world will be sunk in misery and poverty. The nations will all decline in a catastrophe that will leave nothing behind that is worth dominating. No one will have gained anything. Everyone will have lost everything.

Once all this is understood, and people generally agree that population growth must not be allowed to continue, they must also come to understand how that growth can be stopped. Population grows because more people are being born than are dying. There are two ways, then, in which the growth can be stopped. You can increase the number of people who die until it matches the number of people who are being born. Or else you can decrease the number of people who are born until it matches the number of people who are dying.

The first method—increasing the death rate—is the usual way in which population is controlled in all species of living things other than ourselves. It is the method by which human populations have been controlled in the past. It is the "natural" method. If there are too many people, some starve or die of disease or by violence. If we don't do anything now, it will be the way population will be controlled in the future. Billions will die.

Must we let that happen because it is the "natural" way?

Through all the history of mankind, the human brain has been bending nature to its will. If we had really decided that the "natural" way was the right way, we would never have begun to make tools or build fires or develop agriculture or study science. It is because mankind has bent nature to its will that there are now many, many people who live more comfortably and better than people ever have before. We must continue to work out ways to be more comfortable by using the intelligent way, and not just the "natural" way.

The "natural" way to control population is by raising the death rate, but we don't want that, for catastrophe lies that way. The intelligent way is to reduce the birth rate. If, say, 40,000,000 people die each year, then not more than 40,000,000 people should be born each year. In fact, we may want to *reduce* the world population to some reasonable value, in which case, if 40,000,000 people die each year, we may want only 30,000,000 people to be born, or only 20,000,000, till the desired population level is reached.

But how can the birth rate be reduced?

One way is for people to stop mating. This, however, is not very practical, since people enjoy it too much to stop. A better way is to let mating continue but to use methods that keep it from resulting in[2] babies.

There are a number of different ways in which the birth rate can be made to drop without interfering with people's pleasure. In

---

2. 초래하다, 가져오다

the last twenty years, the birth rate in the United States and in some other countries has dropped because more and more women are using pills to keep from having babies they don't want.

To make sure that mating doesn't result in babies is called "birth control." It is by adopting methods of birth control that population growth can be stopped with the least damage.

There are many difficulties here. Certain religious organizations are against birth control. Many groups of people have ways of life that would not fit in easily with birth control. Then, too, even if birth control were desired, there are many places in the world where people are so poor they can't afford to buy the materials that make it possible.

So you see, it comes down to education again. People not only have to be taught that a problem exists, they have to be taught exactly how to solve it by birth control and why it is right to do so. And they must be given the necessary materials without charge.

EXERCISES

A. *Answer the following questions.*

1. What are the myths of some people who don't believe in population control?
2. What should a country do to avoid being dominated by other countries?
3. What will happen if every nation tries to raise its population?
4. What are two ways of stopping the population growth?
5. What are the natural way and intelligent way of controlling population?

6. What are some of the difficulties of birth control?

B. *Write in each blank space a word that fits naturally.*

1. They say that it would ( ) no harm to let the whole world become that densely populated.
2. The country has no forests to speak ( ).
3. They don't realize that science just won't be able to keep ( ) the pace.
4. It's not so ( ) the size of the army as its organization and the technical level of its weapons.
5. You can increase the number of people who die until it matches the number of people who are being ( ).
6. If there are too many people, some starve or die of disease or ( ) violence.
7. We must continue to work ( ) ways to be more comfortable by using the intelligent way.
8. A better way is to let mating continue but to use methods that keep it ( ) resulting in babies.
9. There are a number of different ways ( ) which the birth rate can be made to drop without interfering with people's pleasure.
10. It is by adopting methods of birth control that population growth can be stopped ( ) the least damage.
11. Many groups of people have ways of life that would not fit ( ) easily with birth control.
12. Then, too, even if birth control were desired, there are many places in the world where people are so poor they can't afford to buy the materials that ( ) it possible.
13. The nations will all decline in a catastrophe that will leave nothing behind that is ( ) dominating.

C. *Read the following statements based on the essay. Write T if a statement is true, and F if it is false.*

1. Many people think there is nothing to worry about the world population because there are many scientists working on it.
2. The Netherlands is prosperous because of her large population.
3. The Netherlands has fertile forests and much oil.
4. Strength of a nation is measured by her population.
5. A nation can avoid being dominated by its neighbors by raising its standard of living and its level of technology.
6. The best way in which a nation can try to avoid being dominated by its neighbor is to increase its population.
7. The method of increasing the death rate is the usual way in which population is controlled in all species of living things including ourselves.
8. People think that the best way to control population is by raising the death rate.
9. The Netherlands is much more densely populated than the world average.
10. Even though birth control were desired, the people in certain places in the world are too poor to buy the materials that make it possible.

6. The Abstractions of Beasts

CARL SAGAN*

"***Beasts*** abstract not," announced John Locke[1], expressing mankind's prevailing opinion throughout recorded history: Bishop Berkeley[2] had, however, a sardonic rejoinder: "If the fact that brutes abstract not be made the distinguishing property of that sort of animal, I fear a great many of those that pass for men must be reckoned into their numbers." Abstract thought, at least in its more subtle varieties, is not an invariable accompaniment of everyday life for the average man. Could abstract thought be a matter not of kind but of degree? Could other animals be capable of abstract thought but more rarely or less deeply than humans?

We have the impression that other animals are not very intelligent. But have we examined the possibility of animal intelligence carefully enough, or, as in François Truffaut's poignant film *The Wild Child*, do we simply equate the absence of our style of expression of intelligence with the absence of intelligence? In discussing communication with the animals, the

---

* **Carl Sagan(1934~):** 미국의 우주 과학자 및 저술가로 The Dragons of Eden, The Cosmic Connection등의 저서가 있음

1. 영국의 철학가. An Essay Concerning Human Understanding(1690)등의 작품이 있음
2. Ireland의 철학가로 A Treatise Concerning the Principles of Human Knowledge(1710)등의 작품이 있음

French philosopher Montaigne remarked, "The defect that hinders communication betwixt them and us, why may it not be on our part as well as theirs?"

There is, of course, a considerable body of anecdotal information suggesting chimpanzee intelligence. The first serious study of the behavior of simians—including their behavior in the wild—was made in Indonesia by Alfred Russell Wallace, the co-discoverer of evolution by natural selection. Wallace concluded that a baby orangutan he studied behaved "exactly like a human child in similar circumstances." In fact, "orangutan" is a Malay phrase meaning not ape but "man of the woods." Teuber recounted many stories told by his parents, pioneer German ethologists who founded and operated the first research station devoted to chimpanzee behavior on Tenerife in the Canary Islands early in the second decade of this century. It was here that Wolfgang Kohler performed his famous studies of Sultan, a chimpanzee "genius" who was able to connect two rods in order to reach an otherwise inaccessible banana. On Tenerife, also, two chimpanzees were observed maltreating a chicken: One would extend some food to the fowl, encouraging it to approach; whereupon the other would thrust at it with a piece of wire it had concealed behind its back. The chicken would retreat but soon allow itself to approach once again—and be beaten once again. Here is a fine combination of behavior sometimes thought to be uniquely human : cooperation, planning a future course of action, deception and cruelty. It also reveals that chickens have a very low capacity for avoidance learning.

Until a few years ago, the most extensive attempt to communicate with chimpanzees went something like this: A newborn chimp was taken into a household with a newborn baby, and both would be raised together—twin cribs, twin bassinets, twin high chairs, twin potties, twin diaper pails, twin baby powder cans. At the end of three years, the young chimp had, of course, far outstripped the young human in manual dexterity, running, leaping, climbing and other motor skills. But while the child was happily babbling away, the chimp could say only, and with enormous difficulty, "Mama," "Papa," and "cup." From this it was widely concluded that in language, reasoning and other higher mental functions, chimpanzees were only minimally competent: "Beasts abstract not."

But in thinking over these experiments, two psychologists, Beatrice and Robert Gardner, at the University of Nevada, realized that the pharynx and larynx of the chimp are not suited for human speech. Human beings exhibit a curious multiple use of the mouth for eating, breathing and communication. In insects such as crickets, which call to one another by rubbing their legs, these three functions are performed by completely separate organ systems. Human spoken language seems to be adventitious. The exploitation of organ systems with other functions for communication in humans is also indicative of the comparatively recent evolution of our linguistic abilities. It might be, the Gardners reasoned, that chimpanzees have substantial language abilities which could not be expressed because of the limitations of their anatomy. Was there any symbolic language, they asked, that could employ the strengths rather than the weaknesses of chimpanzee anatomy?

The Gardners hit upon a brilliant idea: Teach a chimpanzee American sign language, known by its acronym Ameslan, and sometimes as "American deaf and dumb language" (the "dumb" refers, of course, to the inability to speak and not to any failure of intelligence). It is ideally suited to the immense manual dexterity of the chimpanzee. It also may have all the crucial design features of verbal languages.

There is by now a vast library of described and filmed conversations, employing Ameslan and other gestural languages, with Washoe, Lucy, Lana and other chimpanzees studied by the Gardners and others. Not only are there chimpanzees with working vocabularies of 100 to 200 words; they are also able to distinguish among nontrivially different grammatical patterns and syntaxes. What is more, they have been remarkably inventive in the construction of new words and phrases.

On seeing for the first time a duck land quacking in a pond, Washoe gestured "waterbird," which is the same phrase used in English and other languages, but which Washoe invented for the occasion. Having never seen a spherical fruit other than an apple, but knowing the signs for the principal colors, Lana, upon spying a technician eating an orange, signed "orange apple". After tasting a watermelon, Lucy described it as "candy drink" or "drink fruit," which is essentially the same word form as the English "water melon." But after she had burned her mouth on her first radish, Lucy forever after described them as "cry hurt food." A small doll placed unexpectedly in Washoe's cup elicited the response "Baby in my drink." When Washoe soiled, particularly clothing or furniture, she was taught the sign "dirty," which she then extrapolated as a general term of abuse. A rhesus monkey that evoked her displeasure was repeatedly signed at: "Dirty monkey, dirty monkey, dirty monkey." Occasionally Washoe would say things like "Dirty Jack, gimme drink." Lana, in a moment of creative annoyance, called her trainer "You green shit." Chimpanzees have invented swear words. Washoe also seems to have a sort of sense of humor; once, when riding on her trainer's shoulders and, perhaps inadvertently, wetting him, she signed: "Funny, funny."

Lucy was eventually able to distinguish clearly the meanings of the phrases "Roger tickle Lucy" and "Lucy tickle Roger," both of which activities she enjoyed with gusto. Likewise, Lana extrapolated from "Tim groom Lana" to "Lana groom Tim." Washoe was observed "reading" a magazine—i.e., slowly turning the pages, peering intently at the pictures and making, to no one in particular, an appropriate sign, such as "cat" when viewing a photograph of a tiger, and "drink" when examining a Vermouth advertisement. Having learned the sign "open" with a door, Washoe extended the concept to a briefcase. She also attempted to converse in Ameslan with the laboratory cat, who turned out to be the only illiterate in the facility. Having acquired this marvelous method of communication, Washoe may have been surprised that the cat was not also competent in Ameslan. And when one day Jane, Lucy's foster mother, left the laboratory, Lucy gazed after her and signed: "Cry me. Me cry."

Boyce Rensberger is a sensitive and gifted reporter for the *New York Times* whose parents could neither speak nor hear, although he is in both respects normal. His first language, however, was Ameslan. He had been abroad on a European assignment for the *Times* for some years. On his return to the United States, one of his first domestic duties was to look into the Gardners' experiments with Washoe. After some little time with the chimpanzee, Rensberger reported, "Suddenly I realized I was conversing with a member of another species in my native tongue." The use of the word tongue is, of course, figurative: it is built deeply into the structure of the language (a word that also means "tongue"). In fact, Rensberger was conversing with a member of another species in his native "hand." And it is just this transition from tongue to hand that has permitted humans to regain the ability—lost, according to Josephus[3], since Eden—to communicate with the animals.

In addition to Ameslan, chimpanzees and other nonhuman primates are being taught a variety of other gestural languages. At the Yerkes Regional Primate Research Center in Atlanta, Georgia, they are learning a specific computer language called (by the humans, not the chimps) "Yerkish." The computer records all of its subjects' conversations, even during the night when no humans are in attendance; and from its ministrations we have learned that chimpanzees prefer jazz to rock and movies about chimpanzees to movies about human beings. Lana had, by January 1976, viewed *The Developmental Anatomy of the Chimpanzees* 245 times. She would undoubtedly appreciate a larger film library.

The machine provides for many of Lana's needs, but not all. Sometimes, in the middle of the night, she forlornly types out: "Please, machine, tickle Lana." More elaborate requests and commentaries, each requiring a creative use of a set grammatical form, have been developed subsequently.

Lana monitors her sentences on a computer display, and erases those with grammatical errors. Once, in the midst of Lana's construction of an elaborate sentence, her trainer mischievously and repeatedly interposed, from his separate computer console, a word that made nonsense of Lana's sentence. She gazed at her computer display, spied her trainer at his console, and composed a new sentence: "Please, Tim, leave room." Just as Washoe and Lucy can be said to speak, Lana can be said to write.

Recent experiments performed by James Dewson of the Stanford University School of Medicine and his colleagues give some physiological support to the idea of language centers in the simian neocortex—in particular, like humans, in the left

---

3. 기원 1세기의 유태인 장군 및 역사가

hemisphere. Monkeys were trained to press a green light when they heard a hiss and a red light when they heard a tone. Some seconds after a sound was heard, the red or the green light would appear at some unpredictable position—different each time—on the control panel. The monkey pressed the appropriate light and, in the case of a correct guess, was rewarded with a pellet of food. Then the time interval between hearing the sound and seeing the light was increased up to twenty seconds. In order to be rewarded, the monkeys now had to remember for twenty seconds which noise they had heard. Dewson's team then surgically excised part of the so-called auditory association cortex from the left hemisphere of the neocortex in the temporal lobe[4]. When retested, the monkeys had very poor recall of which sound they were then hearing. After less than a second they could not recall whether it was a hiss or a tone. The removal of a comparable part of the temporal lobe from the right hemisphere produced no effect whatever on this task. "It looks," Dewson was reported to say, "as if we removed the structure in the monkeys' brains that may be analogous to human language centers." Similar studies on rhesus monkeys, but using visual rather than auditory stimuli, seem to show no evidence of a difference between the hemispheres of the neocortex.

Because adult chimpanzees are generally thought (at least by zoo-keepers) to be too dangerous to retain in a home or home environment, Washoe and other verbally accomplished chimpanzees have been involuntarily "retired" soon after reaching puberty. Thus we do not yet have experience with the adult language abilities of monkeys and apes. One of the most intriguing questions is whether a verbally accomplished chimpanzee mother will be able to communicate language to her offspring. It seems very likely that this should be possible and that

4. 측두엽내의 신피질

a community of chimps initially competent in gestural language could pass down the language to subsequent generations.

Where such communication is essential for survival, there is already some evidence that apes transmit extragenetic or cultural information. Jane Goodall observed baby chimps in the wild emulating the behavior of their mothers and learning the reasonably complex task of finding an appropriate twig and using it to prod into a termite's nest so as to acquire some of these tasty delicacies.

Differences in group behavior—something that it is very tempting to call cultural differences—have been reported among chimpanzees, baboons, macaques and many other primates. For example, one group of monkeys may know how to eat bird's eggs, while an adjacent band of precisely the same species may not. Such primates have a few dozen sounds or cries, which are used for intra-group communication, with such meanings as "Flee; here is a predator." But the sound of the cries differs somewhat from group to group; there are regional accents.

An even more striking experiment was performed accidentally by Japanese primatologists attempting to relieve an overpopulation and hunger problem in a community of macaques on an island in south Japan. The anthropologists threw grains of wheat on a sandy beach. Now it is very difficult to separate wheat grains one by one from sand grains; such an effort might even expend more energy than eating the collected wheat would provide. But one brilliant macaque, Imo, perhaps by accident or out of pique, threw handfuls of the mixture into the water. Wheat floats; sand sinks, a fact that Imo clearly noted. Through the sifting process she was able to eat well (on a diet of soggy wheat, to be sure). While older macaques, set in their ways, ignored her, the younger monkeys appeared to grasp the importance of her discovery, and imitate it. In the next generation, the practice was more widespread; today all macaques on the island are competent at water sifting, an example of a cultural tradition among the monkeys.

Earlier studies on Takasakiyama, a mountain in northeast Kyushu inhabited by macaques, show a similar pattern in cultural evolution. Visitors to Takasakiyama threw caramels wrapped in paper to the monkeys—a common practice in Japanese zoos, but one the Takasakiyama macaques had never before encountered. In the course of play, some young monkeys discovered how to unwrap the caramels and eat them. The habit was passed on successively to their playmates, their mothers, the dominant males (who among the macaques act as baby-sitters for the very young) and finally to the subadult males, who were at the furthest social remove from the monkey children. The process of acculturation took more than three years. In natural primate communities, the existing nonverbal communications are so rich that there is little pressure for the development of a more elaborate gestural language. But if gestural language were necessary for chimpanzee survival, there can be little doubt that it would be transmitted culturally down through the generations.

I would expect a significant development and elaboration of language in only a few generations if all the chimps unable to communicate were to die or fail to produce. Basic English corresponds to about 1,000 words. Chimpanzees are already accomplished in vocabularies exceeding 10 percent of that number. Although a few years ago it would have seemed the most implausible science fiction, it does not appear to me out of the question that, after a few generations in such a verbal chimpanzee community, there might emerge the memoirs of the natural history and mental life of a chimpanzee, published in English or Japanese (with perhaps an "as told to" after the by-line).

If chimpanzees have consciousness, if they are capable of abstractions, do they not have what until now has been described as "human rights"? How smart does a chimpanzee have to be before killing him constitutes murder? What further properties must he show before religious missionaries must consider him worthy of attempts at conversion?

I recently was escorted through a large primate research laboratory by its director. We approached a long corridor lined, to the vanishing point as in a perspective drawing[5], with caged chimpanzees. They were one, two or three to a cage, and I am sure the accommodations were exemplary as far as such institutions (or for that matter traditional zoos) go. As we approached the nearest cage, its two inmates bared their teeth and with incredible accuracy let fly great sweeping arcs of spittle, fairly drenching the lightweight suit of the facility's director. They then uttered a staccato of short shrieks, which echoed down the corridor to be repeated and amplified by other caged chimps, who had certainly not seen us, until the corridor fairly shook with the screeching and banging and rattling of bars. The director informed me that not only spit is apt to fly in such a situation; and at his urging we retreated.

I was powerfully reminded of those American motion pictures of the 1930s and '40s, set in some vast and dehumanized state or federal penitentiary, in which the prisoners banged their eating utensils against the bars at the appearance of the tyrannical warden. These chimps are healthy and well-fed. If they are "only" animals, if they are beasts which abstract not, then my comparison is a piece of sentimental foolishness. But chimpanzees *can* abstract. Like other mammals, they are capable of strong emotions. They have certainly committed no crimes. I do not claim to have the answer, but I think it is certainly worthwhile to raise the question: Why, exactly, all over the civilized world, in

---

5. 투시화법의 소멸점

virtually every major city, are apes in prison?

For all we know, occasional viable crosses between humans and chimpanzees are possible. The natural experiment must have been tried very infrequently, at least recently. If such off-spring are ever produced, what will their legal status be? The cognitive abilities of chimpanzees force us, I think, to raise searching questions about the boundaries of the community of beings to which special ethical considerations are due, and can, I hope, help to extend our ethical perspectives downward through the taxa on Earth and upwards to extraterrestrial organisms, if they exist.

EXERCISES

A. *Answer the following questions.*

1. Do you think animals are capable of abstract thought? Give examples.
2. Do the adult chimpanzees pass down gestural language to their subsequent generations?
3. What do you think of the author's contention that there are regional accents among chimpanzee groups?
4. What does the author give as an example of a cultural tradition among the monkeys?
5. What does the author think about the apes in cages?

B. *Write in each blank space a word that fits naturally.*

1. If the fact be made the distinguishing property of that sort of animal, a great many of those that pass (　　) men must be

reckoned into their numbers.

2. Wallace concluded that a baby orangutan he studied behaved "exactly like a human child (　　) similar circumstances."
3. It also reveals that chickens have a very low capacity (　　) avoidance learning.
4. Until a few years ago, the most extensive attempt to communicate with chimpanzees went something (　　) this.
5. From this (　　) was widely concluded that in language, chimpanzees were only minimally competent.
6. The Gardners hit (　　) a brilliant idea: Teach a chimpanzee American sign language.
7. (　　) his return to the United States, one of his first domestic duties was to look into the Gardners' experiments with Washoe.
8. The cat turned (　　) to be the only illiterate in the facility.
9. Recent experiments give some physiological support (　　) the idea of language centers in the simian neocortex.
10. The monkey pressed the appropriate light and, in the case of a correct guess, was rewarded (　　) a pellet of food.
11. Such an effort might even expend more energy (　　) eating the collected wheat would provide.

C. *Fill in the blanks with the proper forms of the words given.*

1. The "dumb" refers, of course, to the (able) to speak and not to any failure of intelligence.
2. What is more, they have been remarkably (invent) in the construction of new words and phrases.
3. Abstract thought is not an invariable (accompany) of everyday life for the average man.
4. There is a considerable body of (anecdote) information

suggesting chimpanzee intelligence.

5. A chimpanzee "genius" was able to connect two rods in order to reach an otherwise (access) banana.
6. The exploitation of organ systems with other functions for communication in humans is also (indication) of the comparatively recent evolution of our linguistic abilities.
7. Having never seen a (sphere) fruit other than an apple, Lana signed "orange apple".
8. A small doll placed (expect) in Washoe's cup elicited the response "Baby in my drink."
9. In addition to Ameslan, chimpanzees and other nonhuman primates are being taught a variety of other (gesture) languages.
10. The computer records all of its subjects' conversations, even during the night when no humans are in (attend).
11. The (remove) of a comparable part of the temporal lobe from the right hemisphere produced no effect whatever on this task.
12. Where such communication is (essence) for survival, there is already some evidence that apes transmit extragenetic or cultural information.

7. I Have a Dream

MARTIN LUTHER KING, Jr.*

Five score years ago, a great American, in whose symbolic shadow we stand, signed the Emancipation Proclamation[1]. This momentous decree came as a great beacon light of hope to millions of Negro slaves who had been seared in the flames of withering injustice. It came as a joyous daybreak to end the long night of captivity.

But one hundred years later, we must face the tragic fact that the Negro is still not free. One hundred years later, the life of the Negro is still sadly crippled by the manacles of segregation and the chains of discrimination. One hundred years later, the Negro lives on a lonely island of poverty in the midst of a vast ocean of material prosperity. One hundred years later, the Negro is still languishing in the corners of American society and finds himself an exile in his own land. So we have come here today to dramatize an appalling condition.

In a sense we have come to our nation's capital to cash a check. When the architects of our republic wrote the magnificent words of

---

* **Martin Luther King, Jr(1929～1968):** 미국의 흑인 목사, 민권운동가. 이 연설은 1963년 8월 28일 Washington의 민권 시위운동에서 행한 것임. 1964년에 Nobel 평화상 수상. 1968년 4월 4일에 피살 당함.

1. Lincoln 대통령의 노예해방령

the Constitution and the Declaration of Independence, they were signing a promissory note to which every American was to fall heir. This note was a promise that all men would be guaranteed the unalienable rights of life, liberty and the pursuit of happiness.

It is obvious today that America has defaulted on this promissory note insofar as her citizens of color are concerned. Instead of honoring this sacred obligation, America has given the Negro people a bad check[2] ; a check which has come back marked "insufficient funds." But we refuse to believe that the bank of justice is bankrupt. We refuse to believe that there are insufficient funds in the great vaults of opportunity of this Nation. So we have come to cash this check—a check that will give us upon demand the riches of freedom and the security of justice. We have also come to this hallowed spot to remind America of the fierce urgency of *now*. This is no time to engage in the luxury of cooling off or to take the tranquilizing drugs of gradualism. *Now* is the time to make real[3] the promises of Democracy. *Now* is the time to rise from the dark and desolate valley of segregation to the sunlit path of racial justice. *Now* is the time to open the doors of opportunity to all of God's children. *Now* is the time to lift our nation from the quicksands[4] of racial injustice to the solid rock of brotherhood.

It would be fatal for the nation to overlook the urgency of the moment and to underestimate the determination of the Negro. This sweltering summer of the Negro's legitimate discontent will not pass until there is an invigorating autumn of freedom and equality. 1963 is not an end but a beginning. Those who hope that the Negro

---

2. 부도수표
3. realize
4. 流砂, 방심해서는 안되는 위급한 상태

needed to blow off steam[5] and will now be content will have a rude awakening if the nation returns to business as usual. There will be neither rest nor tranquillity in America until the Negro is granted his citizenship rights. The whirlwinds of revolt will continue to shake the foundations of our nation until the bright day of justice emerges.

But there is something that I must say to my people who stand on the warm threshold which leads into the palace of justice. In the process of gaining our rightful place we must not be guilty of wrongful deeds. Let us not seek to satisfy our thirst for freedom by drinking from the cup of bitterness and hatred. We must forever conduct our struggle on the high plane of dignity and discipline. We must not allow our creative protest to degenerate into physical violence. Again and again we must rise to the majestic heights of meeting physical force with soul force. The marvelous new militancy which has engulfed the Negro community must not lead us to a distrust of all white people, for many of our white brothers, as evidenced by their presence here today, have come to realize that their destiny is tied up with our destiny and their freedom is inextricably bound to our freedom. We cannot walk alone.

And as we walk, we must make the pledge that we shall march ahead. We cannot turn back. There are those who are asking the devotees of civil rights, "When will you be satisfied?" We can never be satisfied as long as the Negro is the victim of the unspeakable horrors of police brutality. We can never be satisfied as long as our bodies, heavy with the fatigue of travel, cannot gain lodging in the motels of the highways and the hotels of the cities. We cannot be satisfied as long as the Negro's basic mobility is from a smaller ghetto to a larger one. We can never be satisfied as long as a Negro

---

5. 불평을 토로하다

in Mississippi cannot vote and a Negro in New York believes he has nothing for which to vote. No, no, we are not satisfied, and we will not be satisfied until justice rolls down like waters and righteousness like a mighty stream.

I am not unmindful that some of you have come here out of great trials and tribulations. Some of you have come fresh from narrow jail cells. Some of you have come from areas where your quest for freedom left you battered by the storms of persecution and staggered by the winds of police brutality. You have been the veterans of creative suffering. Continue to work with the faith that unearned suffering is redemptive.

Go back to Mississippi, go back to Alabama, go back to South Carolina, go back to Georgia, go back to Louisiana, go back to the slums and ghettos of our northern cities, knowing that somehow this situation can and will be changed. Let us not wallow in the valley of despair.

I say to you today, my friends, that in spite of the difficulties and frustrations of the moment I still have a dream. It is a dream deeply rooted in the American dream.

I have a dream that one day this nation will rise up and live out[6] the true meaning of its creeds: "We hold these truths to be self-evident; that all men are created equal."

I have a dream that one day on the red hills of Georgia the sons of former slaves and the sons of former slaveowners will be able to sit down together at the table of brotherhood.

I have a dream that one day even the state of Mississippi, a desert state sweltering with the heat of injustice and oppression, will be transformed into an oasis of freedom and justice.

---

6. 실천하다

I have a dream that my four little children will one day live in a nation where they will not be judged by the color of their skin, but by the content of their character.

I have a dream today.

I have a dream that one day the state of Alabama, whose governor's lips are presently dripping with the words of interposition and nullification, will be transformed into a situation where little black boys and black girls will be able to join hands with little white boys and white girls and walk together as sisters and brothers.

I have a dream today.

I have a dream that one day every valley shall be exalted, every hill and mountain shall be made low, the rough places will be made plain, and the crooked places will be made straight, and the glory of the Lord shall be revealed, and all flesh[7] shall see it together.

This is our hope. This is the faith with which I return to the South. With this faith we will be able to hew out of the mountain of despair a stone of hope. With this faith we will be able to transform the jangling discords of our nation into a beautiful symphony of brotherhood. With this faith we will be able to work together, to pray together, to struggle together, to go to jail together, to stand up for[8] freedom together, knowing that we will be free one day.

This will be the day when all of God's children will be able to sing with new meaning

> My country, 'tis of thee,
> Sweet land of liberty,
> Of thee I sing:
> Land where my fathers died,

---

7. 모든 중생, 모든 인간
8. 지지하다

Land of the Pilgrim's pride,
From every mountain-side
Let freedom ring.

And if America is to be a great nation this must become true. So let freedom ring from the prodigious hilltops of New Hampshire. Let freedom ring from the mighty mountains of New York. Let freedom ring from the heightening Alleghenies of Pennsylvania!

Let freedom ring from the snowcapped Rockies of Colorado!

Let freedom ring from the curvaceous peaks of California!

But not only that; let freedom ring from Stone Mountain of Georgia!

Let freedom ring from Lookout Mountains of Tennessee!

Let freedom ring from every hill and molehill[9] of Mississippi. From every mountainside, let freedom ring.

When we let freedom ring, when we let it ring from every village and every hamlet, from every state and every city, we will be able to speed up that day when all of God's children, black men and white men, Jews and Gentiles, Protestants and Catholics, will be able to join hands and sing in the words of the old Negro spiritual[10] , "Free at last! free at last! thank God almighty, we are free at last!"

---

9. 작은 언덕
10. 흑인 영가

EXERCISES

A. *Answer the following questions.*

1. What does the phrase "to come to our nation's capital to cash check" mean?
2. Why can't the Negroes be satisfied?
3. Does Dr King instigate the crowd to rise against the injustice?
4. What does Dr King want the government to do for the black people?
5. What must be done if America is to be a great nation?

B. *Write in each blank space a word that fits naturally.*

1. So we have come to cash this check—a check that will give us (   ) demand the riches of freedom and the security of justice.
2. With this faith we will be able to hew (   ) of the mountain of despair a stone of hope.
3. With this faith we will be able to work together, to pray together, to struggle together, to go to jail together, to stand (   ) for freedom together, knowing that we will be free one day.
4. They were signing a promissory note to which every American was to fall (   ).
5. In the process of gaining our rightful place we must not be guilty (   ) wrongful deeds.
6. Their freedom is inextricably bound (   ) our freedom.
7. I have a dream that one day this nation will rise up and live (   ) the true meaning of its creeds.

C. *Write in each blank a suitable word that has one of the following meanings.*

a. The state of being vested with the rights, privileges, and duties of a citizen
b. state of being successful
c. the quality or state of being righteous
d. not enough
e. of very great importance or seriousness
f. the act or system of treating different groups or people in different ways
g. the ability to make firm decisions and act in accordance with them
h. extreme dislike
i. the act of persecuting
j. full of joy or causing joy
k. that cannot be given away

1. This (   ) decree came as a great beacon light of hope to millions of Negro slaves who had been seared in the flames of withering injustice.
2. It came as a (   ) daybreak to end the long night of captivity.
3. The life of the Negro is still sadly crippled by the manacles of segregation and the chains of (   ).
4. The Negro lives on a lonely island of poverty in the midst of a vast ocean of material (   ).
5. This note was a promise that all men would be guaranteed the (   ) rights of life, liberty and the pursuit of happiness.

6. We refuse to believe that there are (   ) funds in the great vaults of opportunity of this Nation.
7. It would be fatal for the nation to overlook the urgency of the moment and to underestimate the (   ) of the Negro.
8. There will be neither rest nor tranquillity in America until the Negro is granted his (   ) rights.
9. Let us not seek to satisfy our thirst for freedom by drinking from the cup of bitterness and (   ).
10. We will not be satisfied until justice rolls down like waters and (   ) like a mighty stream.
11. Some of you have come from areas where your quest for freedom left you battered by the storms of (   ).

MISSION ACCOMPLISHED

If you have a good name,
if you are right more often than you are wrong,
if your children respect you,
if your grandchildren are glad to see you,
if your friends can count on you and you can count on them in time of trouble,
if you can face your God and say 'I have done my best,'
then you are a success.

Ann Landers

8. On Not Answering the Telephone

WILLIAM PLOMER*

If, at the end of a conversation, somebody says to me, 'As soon as I know, I'll ring you up', he is taking too much for granted. He is proposing to attempt the impossible. So I have to say, `I'm afraid you can't. You see, I'm not on the telephone. I just haven't got a telephone.'

Reactions to this are various. Some people say, `Oh, you must have a telephone!' as if they thought I had mislaid[1] it somewhere, or forgotten about it. Some people say, `How terribly inconvenient! How can you do without a telephone?' And some say, `Oh, you wise man, how I envy you!' But the usual reaction is astonishment, and although I regard myself as a quiet, conventional sort of character, I find myself being stared at as a wild or willful eccentric, especially when somebody says, `Well, if I can't ring you up, perhaps you'll ring me up', and I reply, `Perhaps; but I'm more likely to write to you.'

Why don't I have a telephone? Not because I pretend to be wise or pose as unusual. There are two chief reasons: because I don't really like the telephone and because I find I can still work

---

* **William Plomer(1903~73):** South Africa의 작가. Four Countries등의 저서가 있음

1. 쉽사리 찾기 어려운 곳에 잘못 두다

and play, eat, breathe and sleep without it. Why don't I like the telephone? Because I think it is a pest and a time-waster. It may create unnecessary suspense and anxiety, as when you wait for an expected call that doesn't come; or irritating delay, as when you keep ringing a number that is always engaged. As for speaking in a public telephone box, that seems to me really horrible. You would not use it unless you were in a hurry, and because you are in a hurry you will find other people waiting before you. When you do get into the box, you are half asphyxiated[2] by stale, unventilated air, flavored with cheap face-powder and chain-smoking; and by the time you have begun your conversation your back is chilled by the cold looks of somebody who is fidgeting to take your place.

If you have a telephone in your own house, you will admit that it tends to ring when you least want it to ring—when you are asleep, or in the middle of a meal or a conversation, or when you are just going out, or when you are in your bath. Are you strong-minded enough to ignore it, to say to yourself, `Ah, well, it will all be the same in a hundred years' time?' You are not. You think there may be some important news or message for you. Have you never rushed dripping from the bath, or chewing from the table, or dazed from the bed, only to be told that you are a wrong number? You were told the truth. In my opinion all telephone numbers are wrong numbers. If, of course, your telephone rings and you decide not to answer it, then you will have to listen to an idiotic bell ringing and ringing in what is supposed to be the privacy of your own house. You might as well buy a bicycle bell and ring it yourself.

2. 질식시키다, 산소를 제거하다

Suppose you ignore the telephone when it rings, and suppose that, for once, somebody has an important message for you. I can assure you that if a message is really important it will reach you sooner or later. Think of the proverb: 'Ill news travels apace'[3]. I must say good news seems to travel just as fast. And think of the saying: 'The truth will out'. It will. But suppose you answer the telephone when it rings. If, when you take off the receiver, you say, 'Hullo!', just think how absurd that is. Why, you might be saying 'Hullo' to a total stranger, a thing you would certainly think twice about before doing in public, if you were English.

But perhaps, when you take off the receiver, you give your number or your name. But you don't even know whom you are giving it to! Perhaps you have been indiscreet enough to have your name and number printed in the telephone directory, a book with a large circulation, a successful book so often reprinted as to make any author envious, a book more in evidence than Shakespeare or the Bible, and found in all sorts of private and public places. By your self-advertisement you have enabled any stranger, bore, intruder, or criminal to engage you in conversation at a moment's notice in what ought to be the privacy of your own home. It serves you right if you find it impossible to escape from some idle or inquisitive chatterbox, or from somebody who wants something for nothing, or from some reporter bent on questioning you about your own affairs or about the private life of some friend who has just eloped or met with a fatal accident.

But, you will say, you need not have your name printed in the telephone directory, and you can have a telephone which is only usable for outgoing calls. Besides, you will say, isn't it important

3. swiftly

to have a telephone in case of sudden emergency—illness, accident, or fire? Of course, you are right, but here in a thickly populated country like England one is seldom far from a telephone in case of dreadful necessity. All the same, I felt an instant sympathy with a well-known actor whom I heard on the radio the other day. He was asked: 'Suppose you were left alone to live on a desert island, and you were allowed to take just one luxury with you, what would you choose?' 'I would take a telephone', he said, 'and I would push the wire into the sand, and my greatest pleasure would be to sit and look at it, and to think: "It will never ring and I shall never have to answer it." '

If, like me, one is without a telephone, somebody is sure to say, 'Oh, but don't you find you have to write an awful lot of letters?' The answer to that is, 'Yes, but I should have to write an awful lot of letters anyway'. This may bring the remark, 'Ah well, if you don't have a telephone, at least you must have a typewriter'. And the answer to that is 'No'.

'What, no telephone and no typewriter! Do please explain why.' Well, I am a professional man of letters, and when I was younger I thought a typewriter would be convenient. I even thought it was necessary, and that editors and publishers would expect anything sent to them to be typewritten. So I bought myself a typewriter and taught myself to type, and for some years I typed away busily. But I did not enjoy typing. I happen to enjoy the act of writing. I enjoy forming letters or words with a pen, and I never could enjoy tapping the keys of a typewriter. There again, there was a bell—only a little bell that rang at the end of each line—but still, a bell. And the fact is, I am not mechanically minded, and the typewriter is a machine. I have never been really drawn to machines. I don't like oiling, cleaning or mending them. I do not enjoy making them work. To control them gives me no sense of power—or not the kind of power that I find interesting. And machines do not like me. When I touch them they tend to break down, get jammed, catch fire, or blow up.

As with telephones and typewriters, so with cars. I obtained my first driving licence in South Africa at the age of seventeen, having been taught to drive in the rush hours in the middle of the busy city of Johannesburg. I needed the car for use in another part of Africa where in those days there was hardly any motor traffic. The actual process of driving soon became automatic, and my sole idea was to get from one place to another as soon as possible. I therefore drove fast, and within a week or two the speedometer was broken. I never had it mended. I was not a reckless driver, I did not lose control of the car, even on rocky or sandy tracks or driving with chains through deep mud. I never killed or injured anybody. But I was bored, and if circumstances had allowed I should have preferred to walk. Nowadays, living in an over-crowded country where traffic is continuously on the increase and often congested, and where driving is controlled by a great many rules and regulations, I feel no temptation whatever to drive a car.

But, you may say, am I not aware that we are living in a machine age? Am I trying to put the clock back? Am I an escapist, a crank[4], a simple-lifer? Not at all. It is a matter of preference, not principle, that I choose, as far as possible, to do without these things—a telephone, a typewriter, and a car. If other people are willing—and they seem entirely willing and even eager—to make and use these machines for my benefit, I am not less willing to let them do so. I am perfectly ready to pay to be driven

4. 괴상한 사람

about in trains, cars, or aircraft, to take lifts instead of walking upstairs, and to use moving staircases instead of unmoving ones. But I do not wish to be dominated by machines. I do not want to oil them, mend them, or clean them. I do not want to feed a typewriter with sheets of paper, to lose the use of my legs by traveling always by car, or to be summoned, with or without warning, by the telephone.

Is there any conclusion to be drawn from my obstinacy and willfulness, my escapism, if you like to call it that? I think perhaps I had better try to justify myself by trying to prove that what I like is good. At least I have proved to myself that what many people think necessary is not necessary at all. I admit that in different circumstances—if I were a tycoon, for instance, or bedridden—I might find a telephone essential. But then if I were a secretary or taxi-driver I should find typewriter or a car essential. Let me put it another way: there are two things for which the English seem to show particular aptitude: one is mechanical invention, the other is literature. My own business happens to be with the use of words—but I see I must now stop using them. I have just been handed a slip of paper to say that somebody is waiting to speak to me on the telephone. I think I had better answer it. After all, one never knows, it may be something important.

EXERCISES

A. *Answer the following questions.*

1. What is the author's opinion of the telephone?
2. Why doesn't he like using a typewriter?

3. Why doesn't he like driving a car?
4. What is his attitude towards machines?
5. Do you consider the author an escapist or a crank?

B. *Find single words in this essay which have roughly the meanings given below.*

1. a person who has an unusual personality
2. a spoken or written piece of information passed from one person to another
3. suffocated, deprived of oxygen
4. a person who talks too much and foolishly
5. run away from home with a lover
6. immovable, tightly squeezed or wedged together
7. the hours at which traffic is busiest
8. overfull, very crowded
9. unusual person, one whose behavior is unconventional
10. wealthy and powerful business man

C. A few common words are followed by the gerund as a direct object. Complete the following sentences.

1. Have you finished ...
2. Would you mind ...
3. If you can't mend it, try ...
4. I shall never forget ...
5. It is necessary to go on ...
6. Do you remember ...
7. We all enjoy ...
8. When did you begin ...
9. Lots of people hate ...
10. I really can't bear ...

D. *Write in each blank space a word that fits naturally.*

1. He is taking too much (   ) granted.
2. Some people say, `How terribly inconvenient! How can you do (   ) a telephone?'
3. I find myself being stared at (   ) a wild or willful eccentric.
4. You would not use it unless you were (   ) a hurry.
5. Have you never rushed dripping from the bath (   ) to be told that you are a wrong number?
6. When you take off the receiver, you give your number or your name. But you don't even know whom you are giving it (   ).
7. By your self-advertisement you have enabled any stranger to engage you in conversation (   ) a moment's notice.
8. Here in a thickly populated country like England one is seldom far (   ) a telephone in case of dreadful necessity.
9. As with telephones and typewriters, (   ) with cars.
10. My sole idea was to get from one place to another as soon as (   ).
11. I was not a reckless driver, and I did not lose control (   ) the car.
12. We live in an over-crowded city where traffic is continuously (   ) the increase.
13. It is a matter of preference, not principle, that I choose to do (   ) these things —a telephone, a typewriter, and a car.
14. Is there any conclusion to be (   ) from my obstinacy and willfulness?
15. There are two things (   ) which the English seem to show particular aptitude.

9. American Men Don't Cry

ASHLEY MONTAGU*

American men don't cry because it is considered unmasculine to do so. Only sissies[1] cry. Crying is a "weakness" characteristic of the female, and no American male wants to be identified with anything in the least weak or feminine. Crying, in our culture, is identified with childishness, with weakness and dependence. No one likes a crybaby, and we disapprove of crying even in children, discouraging it in them as early as possible. In a land so devoted to the pursuit of happiness as ours, crying really is rather un-American. Adults must learn not to cry in situations in which it is permissible for a child to cry. Women being the "weaker" and "dependent" sex, it is only natural that they should cry in certain emotional situations. In women, crying is excusable. But in men, crying is a mark of weakness. So goes the American credo with regard to crying.

"A little man," we impress on our male children, "never cries. Only sissies and crybabies do." And so we condition males in America not to cry whenever they feel like doing so. It is not that

* **Ashley Montagu (1905~):** London에서 태어나 1927년에 미국에 정착하여 Harvard, Princeton등의 대학에서 문화인류학 교수를 역임. 저서에는 The Fallacy of Race(1942), The Natural Superiority of Women등이 있음

1. 나약한 사내, 겁쟁이

American males are unable to cry because of some biological time clock within them which causes them to run down[2] in that capacity as they grow older, but that they are trained not to cry. No "little man" wants to be like that "inferior creature," the female. And the worst thing you can call him is a sissy or a crybaby. And so the "little man" represses his desire to cry and goes on doing so until he is unable to cry even when he wants to. Thus do we produce a trained incapacity in the American male to cry. And this is bad. Why is it bad? Because crying is a natural function of the human organism which is designed to restore the emotionally disequilibrated person to a state of equilibrium. The return of the disequilibrated organ systems of the body to steady states or dynamic stability is known as homeostasis[3]. Crying serves a homeostatic function for the organism as whole. Any interference with homeostatic mechanisms is likely to be damaging to the organism. And there is good reason to believe that the American male's trained incapacity to cry is seriously damaging to him.

It is unnecessary to cry whenever one wants to cry, but one should be able to cry when one ought to cry—when one needs to cry. For to cry under certain emotionally disequilibrating conditions is necessary for the maintenance of health.

To be human is to weep. The human species is the only one in the whole of animated nature that sheds tears. The trained inability of any human being to weep is a lessening of his capacity to be human—a defect which usually goes deeper than the mere inability to cry. And this, among other things, is what American

---

2. 쇠약해지다, 멈추다
3. (심리, 생리) 항상성

parents—with the best intentions in the world—have achieved for the American male. It is very sad. If we feel like it, let us all have a good cry—and clear our minds of those cobwebs of confusion which have for so long prevented us from understanding the ineluctable necessity of crying.

EXERCISES

A. *Answer the following questions.*

1. The author makes an assertion in the first line. How does he support it?
2. The author attributes American men's reluctance to cry not to nature but to environment and training. Does he give evidence to support his view?
3. What do the Americans identify crying with?

B. *Write in each blank space a word that fits naturally.*

1. No American male wants to be identified ( ) anything in the least weak or feminine.
2. We condition males in America not to cry whenever they feel ( ) doing so.
3. He represses his desire to cry and goes on doing so until he is unable to cry even when he wants ( ).
4. The human species is the only one in the whole of animated nature that sheds ( ).
5. Let us all have a good cry—and clear our minds ( ) those cobwebs of confusion.

C. *Fill in the blanks in the following sentences with the proper forms of the words given.*

1. American men don't cry because it is considered (masculine) to do so.
2. Crying is a "weakness" (character) of the female.
3. We disapprove of crying even in children, (courage) it in them as early as possible.
4. In a land so (devote) to the pursuit of happiness as ours, crying really is rather un-American.
5. Adults must learn not to cry in situations in which it is (permit) for a child to cry.

D. *Write in each blank a suitable word that has one of the following meanings.*

a. the tendency to maintain internal stability
b. the act of keeping something in good condition
c. lack of power or ability
d. a state of balance between opposing forces
e. not wanted

1. Thus do we produce a trained ( ) in the American male to cry.
2. The return of the disequilibrated organ systems of the body to steady states or dynamic stability is known as ( ).
3. Crying is a natural function of the human organism which is designed to restore the emotionally disequilibrated person to a state of ( ).
4. It is ( ) to cry whenever one wants to cry, but one should be able to cry when one ought to cry.
5. To cry under certain emotionally disequilibrating conditions is necessary for the ( ) of health.

LIFE

Life is an opportunity, benefit from it.
Life is a beauty, admire it.
Life is bliss, taste it.
Life is a dream, realize it.
Life is a challenge, meet it.
Life is a duty, complete it.
Life is a game, play it.
Life is costly, care for it.
Life is wealth, keep it.
Life is love, enjoy it.
Life is mystery, know it.
Life is a promise, fulfill it.
Life is sorrow, overcome it.
Life is a song, sing it.
Life is a struggle, accept it.
Life is tragedy, confront it.
Life is an adventure, dare it.
Life is luck, make it.
Life is too precious, do not destroy it.
Life is life, fight for it!

Mother Teresa

10. The Virtues of Ambition

JOSEPH EPSTEIN*

Ambition is one of those Rorschach words[1]: define it and you instantly reveal a great deal about yourself. Even that most neutral of works, *Webster's*, in its Seventh New Collegiate Edition, gives itself away[2], defining ambition first and foremost as "an ardent desire for rank, fame, or power." Ardent immediately assumes a heat incommensurate with good sense and stability, and rank, fame, and power have come under fairly heavy attack for at least a century. One can, after all, be ambitious for the public good, for the alleviation of suffering, for the enlightenment of mankind, though there are some who say that these are precisely the ambitious people most to be distrusted.

Surely ambition is behind dreams of glory, of wealth, of love, of distinction, of accomplishment, of pleasure, of goodness. What life does with our dreams and expectations cannot, of course, be predicted. Some dreams, begun in selflessness, end in rancor; other dreams, begun in selfishness, end in large-heartedness. The

---

* **Joseph Epstein(1937～):** 미국의 작가, 교수, 편집인. Marriage in an Age of Possibility (1974)등의 저서가 있음

1. **Hermann Rorschach (1884～1922):** 스위스 정신과 의사가 창시한 여러 가지 모양의 잉크 얼룩을 설명하도록 하여 사람의 마음이나 성격을 판단하는 검사

2. 정체를 들어내다, 자신에 불리한 말을 무심코 하다

unpredictability of the outcome of dreams is no reason to cease dreaming.

To be sure, ambition, the sheer thing unalloyed by some larger purpose than merely clambering up, is never a pretty prospect to ponder. As drunks have done to alcohol, the single-minded have done to ambition—given it a bad name. Like a taste for alcohol, too, ambition does not always allow for easy satiation. Some people cannot handle it; it has brought grief to others, and not merely the ambitious alone. Still, none of this seems sufficient cause for driving ambition under the counter.

What is the worst that can be said — that has been said — about ambition? Here is a (surely) partial list:

To begin with, it, ambition, is often antisocial, and indeed is now outmoded, belonging to an age when individualism was more valued and useful than it is today. The person strongly imbued with ambition ignores the collectivity; socially detached, he is on his own and out for his own[3]. Individuality and ambition are firmly linked. The ambitious individual, far from identifying himself and his fortunes with the group, wishes to rise above it. The ambitious man or woman sees the world as a battle; rivalrousness is his or her principal emotion: the world has limited prizes to offer, and he or she is determined to get his or hers. Ambition is, moreover, jesuitical; it can argue those possessed by it into believing that what they want for themselves is good for everyone—that the satisfaction of their own desires is best for the commonweal. The truly ambitious believe that it is a dog-eat-dog world[4], and they are distinguished by wanting to be the dogs that do the eating.

---

3. 갈구하여, 애써서

4. 치열한 경쟁 세계

From here it is but a short hop to[5] believe that those who have achieved the common goals of ambition—money, fame, power—have achieved them through corruption of a greater or lesser degree, mostly a greater. Thus all politicians in high places, thought to be ambitious, are understood to be, ipso facto[6], without moral scruples. How could they have such scruples—a weighty burden in a high climb—and still have risen as they have?

If ambition is to be well regarded, the rewards of ambition—wealth, distinction, control over one's destiny—must be deemed worthy of the sacrifices made on ambition's behalf. If the tradition of ambition is to have vitality, it must be widely shared; and it especially must be esteemed by people who are themselves admired, the educated not least among them. The educated not least because, nowadays more than ever before, it is they who have usurped the platforms of public discussion and wield the power of the spoken and written word in newspapers, in magazines, on television. In an odd way, it is the educated who have claimed to have given up on ambition as an ideal. What is odd is that they have perhaps most benefited from ambition—if not always their own then that of their parents and grandparents. There is a heavy note of hypocrisy in this; a case of closing the barn door after the horses have escaped—with the educated themselves astride them.

Certainly people do not seem less interested in success and its accouterments now than formerly. Summer homes, European travel, BMWs[7]—the locations, place names and name brands may change, but such items do not seem less in demand today than a

---

5. 한 발로 짧게 뛰는 일, 즉 힘들지 않은 쉬운 일
6. (L.): by that very fact. 사실상
7. a high quality, expensive German car

decade or two years ago. What has happened is that people cannot own up to their dreams, as easily and openly as once they could, lest they be thought pushing, acquisitive, vulgar. Instead we are treated to fine pharisaical spectacles, which now more than ever seem in ample supply: the revolutionary lawyer quartered in the $250,000 Manhattan condominium; the critic of American materialism with a Southampton summer home; the publisher of radical books who takes his meals in three-star restaurants; the journalist advocating participatory democracy in all phases of life, whose own children are enrolled in private schools. For such people and many more perhaps not so egregious, the proper formulation is, "Succeed at all costs but refrain from *appearing* ambitious."

The attacks on ambition are many and come from various angles; its public defenders are few and unimpressive, where they are not extremely unattractive. As a result, the support for ambition as a healthy impulse, a quality to be admired and inculcated in the young, is probably lower than it has ever been in the United States. This does not mean that ambition is at an end, that people no longer feel its stirrings and promptings, but only that, no longer openly honored, it is less often openly professed. Consequences follow from this, of course, some of which are that ambition is driven underground, or made sly, or perverse. It can also be forced into vulgarity, as witness[8] the blatant pratings of its contemporary promoters. Such, then, is the way things stand: on the left angry critics, on the right obtuse supporters, and in the middle, as usual, the majority of earnest people trying to get on in life.

Many people are naturally distrustful of ambition, feeling that it represents something intractable in human nature. Thus John

---

8. ...이 한 예가 된다

Dean entitled his book about his involvement in the Watergate affair during the Nixon administration *Blind Ambition*, as if ambition were to blame for his ignoble actions, and not the constellation of qualities that make up his rather shabby character. Ambition, it must once again be underscored, is morally a two-sided street. Place next to John Dean Andrew Carnegie[9], who, among other philanthropic acts, bought the library of Lord Acton, at a time when Acton was in financial distress, and assigned its custodianship to Acton, who never was told who his benefactor was. Need much more be said on the subject than that, important though ambition is, there are some things that one must not sacrifice to it?

But going at things the other way, sacrificing ambition so as to guard against its potential excesses, is to go at things wrongly. To discourage ambition is to discourage dreams of grandeur and greatness. All men and women are born, live, suffer, and die; what distinguishes us one from another is our dreams, whether they be dreams about worldly or unworldly things, and what we do to make them come about.

It may seem an exaggeration to say that ambition is the linchpin of society, holding many of its disparate elements together, but it is not an exaggeration by much. Remove ambition and the essential elements of society seem to fly apart. Ambition, as opposed to mere fantasizing about desires, implies work and discipline to achieve goals, personal and social, of a kind society cannot survive without. Ambition is intimately connected with family, for men and women not only work partly for their families; husbands and wives are often ambitious for each other, but harbor some of their most ardent ambitions for their children. Yet to have

---

9. **Andrew Carnegie(1835~1919):** 미국의 사업가 및 자선가로 강철로 많은 돈을 벌었으나 죽기 전에 대부분을 사회에 기부하였음

a family nowadays—with birth control readily available, and inflation a good economic argument against having children—is nearly an expression of ambition in itself. Finally, though ambition was once the domain chiefly of monarchs and aristocrats, it has, in more recent times, increasingly become the domain of the middle classes. Ambition and futurity—a sense of building for tomorrow—are inextricable. Working, saving, planning—these, the daily aspects of ambition—have always been the distinguishing marks of a rising middle class. The attack against ambition is not incidentally an attack on the middle class and what it stands for. Like it or not, the middle class has done much of society's work in America; and it, the middle class, has from the beginning run on ambition.

It is not difficult to imagine a world shorn of ambition. It would probably be a kinder world: without demands, without abrasions, without disappointments. People would have time for reflection. Such work as they did would not be for themselves but for the collectivity. Competition would never enter in. Conflict would be eliminated, tension become a thing of the past. The stress of creation would be at an end. Art would no longer be troubling, but purely celebratory in its functions. The family would become superfluous as a social unit, with all its former power for bringing about neurosis drained away. Longevity would be increased, for fewer people would die of heart attack or stroke caused by tumultuous endeavor. Anxiety would be extinct. Time would stretch on and on, with ambition long departed from the human heart.

Ah, how unrelievedly boring life would be!

There is a strong view that holds that success is a myth, and ambition therefore a sham. Does this mean that success does not really exist? That achievement is at bottom empty? That the efforts of men and women are of no significance alongside the force of movements and events? Now not all success, obviously, is worth esteeming, nor all ambition worth cultivating. Which are and which are not is something one soon enough learns on one's own. But even the most cynical secretly admit that success exists; that achievement counts for a great deal; and that the true myth is that the actions of men and women are useless. To believe otherwise is to take on a point of view that is likely to be deranging. It is, in its implications, to remove all motive for competence, interest in attainment, and regard for posterity.

We do not choose to be born. We do not choose our parents. We do not choose our historical epoch, the country of our birth or the immediate circumstances of our upbringing. We do not, most of us, choose to die; nor do we choose the time or conditions of our death. But within all this realm of choicelessness, we do choose how we shall live: courageously or in cowardice, honorably or dishonorably, with purpose or in drift. We decide what is important and what is trivial in life. We decide that what makes us significant is either what we do or what we refuse to do. But no matter how indifferent the universe may be to our choices and decisions, these choices and decisions are ours to make. We decide. We choose. And as we decide and choose, so are our lives formed. In the end, forming our own destiny is what ambition is about.

One of the qualities that separate us two-legged animals from the four-legged ones is compassion. It is what makes us stand up tall instead of crawling about on all four. And standing up tall is what frees our arms to reach out to a fellow being and say, 'Let me help you.'

EXERCISES

A *Answer the following questions.*

1. What is the dictionary definition of 'ambition'?
2. What does the ambitious individual like to do?
3. How is ambition honored nowadays?
4. What did Andrew Carnegie do to Lord Acton?
5. What roles does ambition play in our lives?

B. *Fill in the blanks with suitable words with the meanings given below.*

a. act of making easier to endure
b. a feeling of bitter unforgiving hatred
c. an important part which keeps the whole thing together
d. the idea that the rights and freedom of the individual are the most important rights in a society
e. enough or more than enough

1. One can be ambitious for the (   ) of suffering of other people.
2. Some dreams, begun in selflessness, end in (   ).
3. It is said that ambition is the (   ) of society, holding many of its disparate elements together.
4. Ambition is often antisocial, and indeed is now outmoded, belonging to an age when (   ) was more valued and useful than it is today.
5. Instead we are treated to fine pharisaical spectacles, which now more than ever seem in (   ) supply.

C. *Give the proper forms of the words given in brackets.*

1. The (predict) of the outcome of dreams is no reason to cease dreaming.
2. The ambitious man or woman sees the world as a battle; (rival) is his or her principal emotion.
3. The children of the journalist advocating (participate) democracy in all phases of life are enrolled in private schools.
4. Ambition can argue those possessed by it into (belief) that what they want for themselves is good for everyone.
5. But going at things the other way, (sacrifice) ambition so as to guard against its potential excesses, is to go at things wrongly.

D. *Fill in the blanks with suitable prepositions.*

1. The ambitious individual, far (   ) identifying himself with the group, wishes to rise above it.
2. Yet to have a family nowadays—(   ) birth control readily available, and inflation a good economic argument (   ) having children—is nearly an expression of ambition in itself.
3. The attack against ambition is not incidentally an attack on the middle class and what it stands (   ).
4. It is not difficult to imagine a world shorn (   ) ambition.
5. In the end, forming our own destiny is what ambition is (   ).

11. The Importance of Loafing

LIN YUTANG*

Culture, as I understand it, is essentially a product of leisure. The art of culture is therefore essentially the art of loafing. From the Chinese point of view, the man who is wisely idle is the most cultured man. For there seems to be a philosophic contradiction between being busy and being wise. Those who are wise won't be busy, and those who are too busy can't be wise. The wisest man is therefore he who loafs most gracefully. Here I shall try to explain, not the technique and varieties of loafing as practiced in China, but rather the philosophy which nourishes this divine desire for loafing in China and gives rise to that carefree, idle, happy-go-lucky[1]—and often poetic—temperament in the Chinese scholars, and to a lesser extent, in the Chinese people in general. How did that Chinese temperament—that distrust of achievement and success and that intense love of living as such—arise?

In the first place, the Chinese theory of leisure, as expressed by a comparatively unknown author of the eighteenth century, Shu Paihsiang, who happily achieved oblivion, is as follows: time is useful because it is not being used. "Leisure in time is like

---

***Lin Yutang(林語堂: 1895～1976):** 중국의 저명한 저술가, 비평가

1. 태평스러운, easygoing

unoccupied floor space in a room." Every working girl who rents a small room where every inch of space is fully utilized feels highly uncomfortable because she has no room to move about, and the moment she gets a raise in salary, she moves into a bigger room where there is a little more unused floor space, besides those strictly useful spaces occupied by her single bed, her dressing table and her two-burner gas range. It is that unoccupied space which makes a room habitable, as it is our leisure hours which make life endurable. I understand there is a rich woman living on Park Avenue, who bought up a neighboring lot to prevent anybody from erecting a skyscraper next to her house. She is paying a big sum of money in order to have space fully and perfectly made useless, and it seems to me she never spent her money more wisely.

In this connection, I might mention a personal experience. I could never see the beauty of skyscrapers in New York, and it was not until I went to Chicago that I realized that a skyscraper could be very imposing and very beautiful to look at, if it had a good frontage and at least half a mile of unused space around it. Chicago is fortunate in this respect, because it has more space than Manhattan. The tall buildings are better spaced, and there is the possibility of obtaining an unobstructed view of them from a long distance. Figuratively speaking, we, too, are so cramped in our life that we cannot enjoy a free perspective of the beauties of our spiritual life. We lack spiritual frontage....

To the Chinese, therefore, with the fine philosophy that "Nothing matters to a man who says nothing matters," Americans offer a strange contrast. Is life really worth all the bother, to the extent of making our soul a slave to the body? The high spirituality of the philosophy of loafing forbids it. The most characteristic advertisement I ever saw was one by an engineering firm with the big words: "Nearly Right Is Not Enough." The desire for one hundred per cent efficiency seems almost obscene. The trouble with Americans is that when a thing is nearly right, they want to make it still better while for a Chinese, nearly right is good enough.

The three great American vices seem to be efficiency, punctuality and the desire for achievement and success. They are the things that make the Americans so unhappy and so nervous. They steal from them their inalienable right of loafing and cheat them of many a good, idle and beautiful afternoon. One must start out with a belief that there are no catastrophes in this world, and that besides the noble art of getting things done, there is a nobler art of leaving things undone. On the whole, if one answers letters promptly, the result is about as good or as bad as if he had never answered them at all. After all, nothing happens, and while one may have missed a few good appointments, one may have also avoided a few unpleasant ones. Most of the letters are not worth answering, if you keep them in your drawer for three months; reading them three months afterwards, one might realize how utterly futile and what a waste of time it would have been to answer them all. Writing letters really can become a vice. It turns our writers into fine promotion salesmen and our college professors into good efficient business executives. In this sense, I can understand Thoreau's contempt for the American who always goes to the post office.

Our quarrel is not that efficiency gets things done and very well done, too. I always rely on American water-taps, rather than on those made in China, because American water-taps do not leak. That is a consolation. Against the old contention, however, that we must all be useful, be efficient, become officials and have power, the old reply is that there are always enough fools left in the world who are willing to be useful, be busy and enjoy power, and so somehow the business of life can and will be carried on. The only point is who are the wise, the loafers or the hustlers? Our quarrel with efficiency is not that it gets things done, but that it is a thief of time when it leaves us no leisure to enjoy ourselves and that it frays our nerves in trying to get things done perfectly. An American editor worries his hair gray to see that no typographical mistakes appear on the pages of his magazine. The Chinese editor is wiser than that. He wants to leave his readers the supreme satisfaction of discovering a few typographical mistakes for themselves. More than that, a Chinese magazine can begin printing serial fiction and forget about it halfway. In America it might bring the roof down on the editors, but in China it doesn't matter, simply because it doesn't matter. American engineers in building bridges calculate so finely and exactly as to make the two ends come together within one-tenth of an inch. But when two Chinese begin to dig a tunnel from both sides of a mountain, both come out on the other side. The Chinese's firm conviction is that it doesn't matter so long as a tunnel is dug through, and if we have two instead of one, why, we have a double track to boot[2]. Provided you are not in a hurry, two tunnels are as good as one, dug somehow, finished somehow and if the train can get through somehow. And the Chinese are extremely punctual, provided you give them plenty of time to do a thing. They always finish a thing on schedule, provided the schedule is long enough.

The tempo of modern industrial life forbids this kind of glorious and magnificent idling. But worse than that, it imposes

2. as well

upon us a different conception of time as measured by the clock, and eventually turns the human being into a clock himself. This sort of thing is bound to come to China, as is evident for instance in a factory of twenty thousand workers. The luxurious prospect of twenty thousand workers coming in at their own sweet pleasure at all hours is, of course, somewhat terrifying. Nevertheless, this is what makes life so hard and hectic. A man who has to be punctually at a certain place at five o'clock has the whole afternoon from one to five ruined for him already. Every American adult is arranging his time on the pattern of the schoolboy—three o'clock for this, five o'clock for that, six-thirty for change of dress; six-fifty for entering the taxi and seven o'clock for emerging into a hotel room. It just makes life not worth living.

And Americans have now come to such a sad state that they are booked up not only for the following day, or the following week, but even for the following month. An appointment three weeks ahead of time is a thing unknown in China. And when a Chinese receives an invitation card, happily he never has to say whether he is going to be present or not. He can put down on the invitation list "coming" if he accepts, or "thanks" if he declines, but in the majority of cases the invited party merely writes the word "know," which is a statement of fact that he knows of the invitation and not a statement of intention. An American or a European leaving Shanghai can tell me that he is going to attend a committee meeting in Paris on April 19, at three o'clock and that he will be arriving in Vienna on May 21 by the seven o'clock train. If an afternoon is to be condemned and executed, must we announce its execution so early? Cannot a fellow travel and be lord of himself, arriving when he likes and taking departure when he likes?

But above all, the American's inability to loaf comes directly from his desire for doing things and in his placing action above being. We should demand that there be character in our lives as we demand there be character in all great art worthy of the name. Unfortunately, character is not a thing which can be manufactured overnight. Like the quality of mellowness in wine, it is acquired by standing still and by the passage of time. The desire of American old men and women for action, trying in this way to gain their self-respect and the respect of the younger generation, is what makes them look so ridiculous to an Oriental. Too much action in an old man is like a broadcast of jazz music from a megaphone on top of an old cathedral. Is it not sufficient that the old people are something? Is it necessary that they must be forever doing something? The loss of the capacity for loafing is bad enough in men of middle age, but the same loss in old age is a crime committed against human nature.

Character is always associated with something old and takes time to grow, like the beautiful facial lines of a man in middle age, lines that are the steady imprint of the man's evolving character. It is somewhat difficult to see character in a type of life where every man is throwing away his last year's car and trading it in for the new model. As are the things we make, so are we ourselves.... We love old cathedrals, old furniture, old silver, old dictionaries and old prints, but we have entirely forgotten about the beauty of old men. I think an appreciation of that kind of beauty is essential to our life, for beauty, it seems to me, is what is old and mellow and well-smoked.

Sometimes a prophetic vision comes to me, a beautiful vision of a millennium when Manhattan will go slow, and when the

American "go-getter[3]" will become an Oriental loafer. American gentlemen will float in skirts and slippers and amble on the side walks of Broadway with their hands in their pockets, if not with both hands stuck in their sleeves in the Chinese fashion. Policemen will exchange a word of greeting with the slow-devil at the crossings, and the drivers themselves will stop and accost each other and inquire after their grandmothers' health in the midst of traffic. Someone will be brushing his teeth outside his shopfront, talking the while placidly with his neighbors, and once in a while, an absent-minded scholar will sail by with a limp volume rolled up and tucked away in his sleeve. Lunch counters will be abolished, and people will be lolling and lounging in soft, low armchairs in an Automat[4] , while others will have learned the art of killing a whole afternoon in some cafe. A glass of orange juice will last half an hour, and people will learn to sip wine by slow mouthfuls, punctuated by delightful, chatty remarks, instead of swallowing it at a gulp. Registration in a hospital will be abolished, "emergency wards" will be unknown, and patients will exchange their philosophy with their doctors. Fire engines will proceed at a snail's pace, their staff stopping on the way to gaze at and dispute over the number of passing wild geese in the sky. It is too bad that there is no hope of this kind of millennium on Manhattan ever being realized. There might be so many more perfect idle afternoons.

3. 수단꾼, 수완가, thruster
4. 50~60년대 성행했던 자동판매기 사용 식당

EXERCISES

A. *Answer the following questions.*

1. What are three great American vices?
2. How does the writer define 'a wise man'?
3. Why does the writer find efficiency disagreeable?
4. Why are Americans unable to loaf?
5. What does the writer try to emphasize in this essay?
6. Elaborate on the sentence "Leisure in time is like unoccupied floor space in a room".

B. *Fill in the blanks with suitable words.*

1. The philosophy gives rise (   ) that carefree, idle, happy-go-lucky temperament in the Chinese scholars.
2. In the first (   ), the Chinese theory of leisure is as follows: time is useful because it is not being used.
3. A rich woman bought up a neighboring lot to prevent anybody (   ) erecting a skyscraper next to her house.
4. It was not until I went to Chicago (   ) I realized that a skyscraper could be very imposing and very beautiful to look at.
5. There is the possibility of obtaining an unobstructed view (   ) them from a long distance.
6. The trouble (   ) Americans is that when a thing is nearly right, they want to make it still better.
7. They steal from them their inalienable right of loafing and cheat them (   ) many a good, idle and beautiful afternoon.
8. One must start out with a belief that besides the noble art of getting things done, there is a nobler art of leaving things

(   ).

9. An American editor worries his hair gray to (   ) that no typographical mistakes appear on the pages of his magazine.
10. They always finish a thing (   ) schedule, provided the schedule is long enough.
11. Americans have now come to such a sad state that they are booked (   ) not only for the following day but even for the following month.
12. The American's inability to loaf comes directly from his desire for doing things and in his placing action (   ) being.
13. We should demand that there be character in our lives as we demand there be character in all great art worthy of the (   ).
14. It is somewhat difficult to see character in a type of life where every man is throwing away his last year's car and trading it in (   ) the new model.

C. *Fill in each blank with a suitable word that has one of the following meanings.*

a. quality or state of being punctual
b. not of any use
c. incapable of producing any result
d. direct opposition between things compared
e. capable of being endured
f. artistic and other activity of the mind, and the works produced by this

1. The art of (   ) is therefore essentially the art of loafing.

2. There seems to be a philosophic ( ) between being busy and being wise.
3. It is that unoccupied space which makes a room habitable, as it is our leisure hours which make life ( ).
4. She is paying a big sum of money in order to have space fully and perfectly made ( ).
5. The three great American vices seem to be efficiency, ( ) and the desire for achievement and success.
6. Reading them three months afterwards, one might realize how utterly ( ) it would have been to answer them all.

ENOUGH

Health enough to make work a pleasure,
Wealth enough to support your needs,
Strength enough to battle with difficulties and
overcome them,
Grace enough to toil until good is accomplished,
Charity enough to see good in your neighbor,
Love enough to move you to be useful and
helpful to others,
Faith enough to make real the things of God,
Hope enough to remove all anxious fears
concerning the future.

Johann Wolfgang von Goethe

12. Shooting an Elephant

GEORGE ORWELL*

In Moulmein, in Lower Burma, I was hated by large numbers of people—the only time in my life that I have been important enough for this to happen to me. I was sub-divisional police officer of the town, and in an aimless, petty kind of way anti-European feeling was very bitter. No one had the guts to raise a riot, but if a European woman went through the bazaars alone somebody would probably spit betel juice[1] over her dress. As a police officer I was an obvious target and was baited whenever it seemed safe to do so. When a nimble Burman tripped me up on the football field and the referee (another Burman) looked the other way, the crowd yelled with hideous laughter. This happened more than once. In the end the sneering yellow faces of young men that met me everywhere, the insults hooted after me when I was at a safe distance, got badly on my nerves[2]. The young Buddhist priests were the worst of all. There were several thousands of them in the town and none of them seemed to have anything to do except stand on street corners and jeer at Europeans.

* **George Orwell (1903～1950):**영국의 소설가, 수필가. 대표작으로는 Animal Farm (1945), Nineteen Eighty-Four (1949)등이 있음.

1. 쓴 빨간 열매를 둘러 싸고 있는 잎으로서 약효가 있기 때문에 씹음
2. 신경을 거슬리게 하다

All this was perplexing and upsetting. For at that time I had already made up my mind that imperialism was an evil thing and the sooner I chucked up[3] my job and got out of it the better. Theoretically—and secretly, of course—I was all for the Burmese and all against their oppressors, the British. As for the job I was doing, I hated it more bitterly than I can perhaps make clear. In a job like that you see the dirty work of Empire at close quarters[4]. The wretched prisoners huddling in the stinking cages of the lockups[5], the grey, cowed faces of the long-term convicts, the scarred buttocks of the men who had been flogged with bamboos —all these oppressed me with an intolerable sense of guilt. But I could get nothing into perspective. I was young and ill-educated and I had had to think out my problems in the utter silence that is imposed on every Englishman in the East. I did not even know that the British Empire is dying, still less did I know that it is a great deal better than the younger empires that are going to supplant it. All I knew was that I was stuck between my hatred of the empire I served and my rage against the evil-spirited little beasts who tried to make my job impossible. With one part of my mind I thought of the British Raj[6] as an unbreakable tyranny, as something clamped down, *in saecula saeculorum*[7], upon the will of prostrate peoples; with another part I thought that the greatest joy in the world would be to drive a bayonet into a Buddhist priest's guts. Feelings like these are normal by-products of imperialism; ask any Anglo-Indian official, if you can catch him off duty.

---

3. give up
4. 아주 가까이서
5. jail
6. British rule
7. for ages and ages

One day something happened which in a roundabout way was enlightening. It was a tiny incident in itself, but it gave me a better glimpse than I had before of the real nature of imperialism—the real motives for which despotic governments act. Early one morning the sub-inspector at a police station the other end of the town rang me up on the 'phone and said that an elephant was ravaging the bazaar. Would I please come and do something about it? I did not know what I could do, but I wanted to see what was happening and I got on to a pony and started out. I took my rifle, an old .44 Winchester[8] and much too small to kill an elephant, but I thought the noise might be useful *in terrorem*[9]. Various Burmans stopped me on the way and told me about the elephant's doings. It was not, of course, a wild elephant, but a tame one which had gone "must.[10]" It had been chained up, as tame elephants always are when their attack of "must" is due, but on the previous night it had broken its chain and escaped. Its mahout[11], the only person who could manage it when it was in that state, had set out in pursuit, but had taken the wrong direction and was now twelve hours' journey away, and in the morning the elephant had suddenly reappeared in the town. The Burmese population had no weapons and were quite helpless against it. It had already destroyed somebody's bamboo hut, killed a cow and raided some fruitstalls and devoured the stock; also it had met the municipal rubbish van and, when the driver jumped out and took to his heels[12], had turned the van over and inflicted violences upon it.

The Burmese sub-inspector and some Indian constables were waiting for me in the quarter where the elephant had been seen. It

8. 윈체스터 연발총
9. 겁내게 하는데는
10. 발정하여 난폭해지다
11. an elephant driver
12. 도망치다

was a very poor quarter, a labyrinth of squalid bamboo huts, thatched with palmleaf, winding all over a steep hillside. I remember that it was a cloudy, stuffy morning at the beginning of the rains. We began questioning the people as to where the elephant had gone and, as usual, failed to get any definite information. That is invariably the case in the East; a story always sounds clear enough at a distance, but the nearer you get to the scene of events the vaguer it becomes. Some of the people said that the elephant had gone in one direction, some said that he had gone in another, some professed not even to have heard of any elephant. I had almost made up my mind that the whole story was a pack of lies, when we heard yells a little distance away. There was a loud, scandalized[13] cry of "Go away, child! Go away this instant!" and an old woman with a switch in her hand came round the corner of a hut, violently shooing away a crowd of naked children. Some more women followed, clicking their tongues and exclaiming; evidently there was something that the children ought not to have seen. I rounded the hut and saw a man's dead body sprawling in the mud. He was an Indian, a black Dravidian[14] coolie, almost naked, and he could not have been dead many minutes. The people said that the elephant had come suddenly upon him round the corner of the hut, caught him with its trunk, put its foot on his back and ground him into the earth. This was the rainy season and the ground was soft, and his face had scored a trench a foot deep and a couple of yards long. He was lying on his belly with arms crucified and head sharply twisted to one side. His face was coated with mud, the eyes wide open, the teeth bared and grinning with an expression of unendurable agony. (Never tell me, by the way, that the dead look peaceful. Most of the corpses I

13. 아연실색한
14. 인도의 고대 종족

have seen looked devilish.) The friction of the great beast's foot had stripped the skin from his back as neatly as one skins a rabbit. As soon as I saw the dead man I sent an orderly to a friend's house nearby to borrow an elephant rifle. I had already sent back the pony, not wanting it to go mad with fright and throw me if it smelt the elephant.

The orderly came back in a few minutes with a rifle and five cartridges, and meanwhile some Burmans had arrived and told us that the elephant was in the paddy fields below, only a few hundred yards away. As I started forward practically the whole population of the quarter flocked out of the houses and followed me. They had seen the rifle and were all shouting excitedly that I was going to shoot the elephant. They had not shown much interest in the elephant when he was merely ravaging their homes, but it was different now that he was going to be shot. It was a bit of fun to them, as it would be to an English crowd; besides they wanted the meat. It made me vaguely uneasy. I had no intention of shooting the elephant—I had merely sent for the rifle to defend myself if necessary—and it is always unnerving to have a crowd following you. I marched down the hill, looking and feeling a fool, with the rifle over my shoulder and an ever-growing army of people jostling at my heels. At the bottom, when you got away from the huts, there was a metalled road and beyond that a miry waste of paddy fields a thousand yards across, not yet ploughed but soggy from the first rains and dotted with course grass. The elephant was standing eighty yards from the road, his left side towards us. He took not the slightest notice of the crowd's approach. He was tearing up bunches of grass, beating them against his knees to clean them and stuffing them into his mouth.

I had halted on the road. As soon as I saw the elephant I knew with perfect certainty that I ought not to shoot him. It is a serious matter to shoot a working elephant—it is comparable to destroying a huge and costly piece of machinery—and obviously one ought not to do it if it can possibly be avoided. And at that distance, peacefully eating, the elephant looked no more dangerous than a cow. I thought then and I think now that his attack of "must" was already passing off; in which case he would merely wander harmlessly about until the mahout came back and caught him. Moreover, I did not in the least want to shoot him. I decided that I would watch him for a little while to make sure that he did not turn savage again, and then go home.

But at that moment I glanced round at the crowd that had followed me. It was an immense crowd, two thousand at least and growing every minute. It blocked the road for a long distance on either side. I looked at the sea of yellow faces above the garish clothes—faces all happy and excited over this bit of fun, all certain that the elephant was going to be shot. They were watching me as they would watch a conjurer about to perform a trick. They did not like me, but with the magical rifle in my hands I was momentarily worth watching. And suddenly I realized that I should have to shoot the elephant after all. The people expected it of me and I had got to do it; I could feel their two thousand wills pressing me forward, irresistibly. And it was at this moment, as I stood there with the rifle in my hands, that I first grasped the hollowness, the futility of the white man's dominion in the East. Here was I, the white man with his gun, standing in front of the unarmed native crowd—seemingly the leading actor of the piece; but in reality I was only an absurd puppet pushed to and fro by the will of those yellow faces behind. I perceived in this moment that when the white man turns tyrant it is his own freedom that he destroys. He becomes a sort of hollow, posing dummy, the conventionalized figure of a sahib[15]. For it is the condition of his

15. European gentleman을 뜻하는 원주민의 표현

rule that he shall spend his life in trying to impress the "natives," and so in every crisis he has got to do what the "natives" expect of him. He wears a mask, and his face grows to fit it. I had got to shoot the elephant. I had committed myself to doing it when I sent for the rifle. A sahib has got to act like a sahib; he has got to appear resolute, to know his own mind and do definite things. To come all that way, rifle in hand, with two thousand people marching at my heels, and then to trail feebly away[16], having done nothing—no, that was impossible. The crowd would laugh at me. And my whole life, every white man's life in the East, was one long struggle not to be laughed at.

But I did not want to shoot the elephant. I watched him beating the bunch of grass against his knees, with that preoccupied grandmotherly air that elephants have. It seemed to me that it would be murder to shoot him. At that age I was not squeamish about killing animals, but I had never shot an elephant and never wanted to. (Somehow it always seems worse to kill a *large* animal.) Besides, there was the beast's owner to be considered. Alive, the elephant was worth at least a hundred pounds; dead, he would only be worth the value of his tusks, five pounds, possibly. But I had got to act quickly. I turned to some experienced-looking Burmans who had been there when we arrived, and asked them how the elephant had been behaving. They all said the same thing: he took no notice of you if you left him alone, but he might charge if you went too close to him.

It was perfectly clear to me what I ought to do. I ought to walk up to within, say, twenty-five yards of the elephant and test his behavior. If he charged, I could shoot; if he took no notice of me, it would be safe to leave him until the mahout came back. But also I knew that I was going to do no such thing. I was a poor shot with

---

16. 힘없이 사라지다

a rifle and the ground was soft mud into which one would sink at every step. If the elephant charged and I missed him, I should have about as much chance as a toad under a steam-roller. But even then I was not thinking particularly of my own skin, only of the watchful yellow faces behind. For at that moment, with the crowd watching me, I was not afraid in the ordinary sense, as I would have been if I had been alone. A white man mustn't be frightened in front of "natives"; and so, in general, he isn't frightened. The sole thought in my mind was that if anything went wrong those two thousand Burmans would see me pursued, caught, trampled on and reduced to a grinning corpse like that Indian up the hill. And if that happened it was quite probable that some of them would laugh. That would never do. There was only one alternative. I shoved the cartridges into the magazine and lay down on the road to get a better aim.

The crowd grew very still, and a deep, low, happy sigh, as of people who see the theatre curtain go up at last, breathed from innumerable throats. They were going to have their bit of fun after all. The rifle was a beautiful German thing with cross-hair sights. I did not then know that in shooting an elephant one would shoot to cut an imaginary bar running from ear-hole to ear-hole. I ought, therefore, as the elephant was sideways on, to have aimed straight at his ear-hole; actually I aimed several inches in front of this, thinking the brain would be further forward.

When I pulled the trigger I did not hear the bang or feel the kick—one never does when a shot goes home—but I heard the devilish roar of glee that went up from the crowd. In that instant, in too short a time, one would have thought, even for the bullet to get there, a mysterious, terrible change had come over the elephant. He neither stirred nor fell, but every line of his body had altered. He looked suddenly stricken, shrunken, immensely old, as though the frightful impact of the bullet had paralysed him without knocking him down. At last, after what seemed a long time—it might have been five seconds, I dare say—he sagged flabbily to his knees. His mouth slobbered. An enormous senility seemed to have settled upon him. One could have imagined him thousands of years old. I fired again into the same spot. At the second shot he did not collapse but climbed with desperate slowness to his feet and stood weakly upright, with legs sagging and head drooping. I fired a third time. That was the shot that did for him. You could see the agony of it jolt his whole body and knock the last remnant of strength from his legs. But in falling he seemed for a moment to rise, for as his hind legs collapsed beneath him he seemed to tower upwards like a huge rock toppling, his trunk reaching skywards like a tree. He trumpeted, for the first and only time. And then down he came, his belly towards me, with a crash that seemed to shake the ground even where I lay.

I got up. The Burmans were already racing past me across the mud. It was obvious that the elephant would never rise again, but he was not dead. He was breathing very rhythmically with long rattling gasps, his great mound of a side painfully rising and falling. His mouth was wide open—I could see far down into caverns of pale pink throat. I waited a long time for him to die, but his breathing did not weaken. Finally I fired my two remaining shots into the spot where I thought his heart must be. The thick blood welled out of him like red velvet, but still he did not die. His body did not even jerk when the shots hit him, the tortured breathing continued without a pause. He was dying, very slowly and in great agony, but in some world remote from me where not even a bullet could damage him further. I felt that I had got to put an end to that dreadful noise. It seemed dreadful to see the great beast lying there, powerless to move and yet powerless to die, and not even to be able to finish him. I sent back for my small rifle and poured shot after shot into his heart and down his throat. They seemed to make no impression. The tortured gasps continued as steadily as the ticking of a clock.

In the end I could not stand it any longer and went away. I heard later that it took him half an hour to die. Burmans were bringing dahs[17] and baskets even before I left, and I was told they had stripped his body almost to the bones by the afternoon.

Afterwards, of course, there were endless discussions about the shooting of the elephant. The owner was furious, but he was only an Indian and could do nothing. Besides, legally I had done the right thing, for a mad elephant has to be killed, like a mad dog, if its owner fails to control it. Among the Europeans opinion was divided. The older men said I was right, the younger men said it was a damn· shame to shoot an elephant for killing a coolie, because an elephant was worth more than any damn Coringhee coolie. And afterwards I was very glad that the coolie had been killed; it put me legally in the right and it gave me a sufficient pretext for shooting the elephant. I often wondered whether any of the others grasped that I had done it solely to avoid looking a fool.

EXERCISES

A. *Answer the following questions.*

1. Do you think this is an autobiographical essay?
2. What does he say about the Burmese social system?
3. What made him shoot the elephant?
4. What are the Burmese feelings towards Europeans?

17. 버마의 백정들이 사용하는 큰 칼

5. What issue does the author address and what kind of evidence is proper to it? Does he actually prove anything?

B. *Write in each blank space a word that fits naturally.*

1. As a police officer I was an obvious target and was baited whenever it seemed safe to (   ) so.
2. The insults hooted after me when I was at a safe distance, got badly (   ) my nerves.
3. Theoretically I was all for the Burmese and all (   ) their oppressors, the British.
4. But I could get nothing (   ) perspective.
5. But it gave me a better glimpse than I had before (   ) the real nature of imperialism.
6. A story always sounds clear enough (   ) a distance, but the nearer you get to the scene of events the vaguer it becomes.
7. The people said that the elephant had come suddenly (   ) him round the corner of the hut.
8. I had no intention (   ) shooting the elephant and it is always unnerving to have a crowd following you.
9. I had committed (   ) to doing it when I sent for the rifle.
10. He took no notice (   ) you if you left him alone, but he might charge if you went too close to him.
11. For at that moment, (   ) the crowd watching me, I was not afraid in the ordinary sense, as I would have been if I had been alone.
12. I felt that I had got to put an (   ) to that dreadful noise.
13. The people expected it (   ) me and I had got to do it; I could feel their two thousand wills pressing me forward.

C. *Choose one of the words that best fits each of the following sentences.*

a. futility	b. pretext	c. bazaar	d. conjurer
e. imperialism	f. discussions	g. rage	h. tyranny
i. squeamish	j. puppet		

1. I had already made up my mind that (   ) was an evil thing and the sooner I chucked up my job and got out of it the better.
2. All I knew was that I was stuck between my hatred of the empire I served and my (   ) against the evil-spirited little beasts.
3. With one part of my mind I thought of the British Raj as an unbreakable (   ).
4. Early one morning the sub-inspector rang me up on the 'phone and said that an elephant was ravaging the (   ).
5. They were watching me as they would watch a (   ) about to perform a trick.
6. It was at this moment that I first grasped the hollowness, the (   ) of the white man's dominion in the East.
7. In reality I was only an absurd (   ) pushed to and fro by the will of those yellow faces behind.
8. At that age I was not (   ) about killing animals.
9. There were endless (   ) about the shooting of the elephant.
10. It put me legally in the right and it gave me a sufficient (   ) for shooting the elephant.

PRAYER OF AN AMERICAN INDIAN

O Great Spirit, whose voice I hear in the winds, and whose breath gives life to all the world, hear me. I am small and weak. I need your strength and wisdom.

Let me walk in beauty and make my eyes ever behold the red and purple sunset.

Make my hands respect the things you have made.

Make my ears sharp to hear your voice.

Make me wise so that I may understand the things you have taught your people.

Let me learn the lessons you have hidden in every leaf and rock.

I seek strength, not to be greater than my brother, but to fight my greatest enemy — myself.

Make me always ready to come to you with clean hands and straight eyes.

So when life fades, as the fading sunset, my spirit may come to you without shame.

13. Return of the Native

SUSAN SCHIEFELBEIN

LADY in a (theater) box: "Is there any culture...in Grover's Corners?"
MR. WEBB: "Well, ma'am, there ain't much...Maybe this is the place to tell you that we've got a lot of pleasures of a kind here: we like the sun comin' up over the mountain in the morning, and we all notice a good deal about the birds...and we watch the change of seasons...."

OUR TOWN

For the first time in fifty years, more Americans are moving to small towns than to cities. In the three decades prior to 1970, nine million people left small towns and moved to urban areas; but in three short years after 1970, 1.5 million left metropolitan areas behind and headed for homes in small towns. Clearly, the once magical attractions of cosmopolitan life—the arts, the sophistication, the promise of success—no longer have the allure of those simple country "pleasures of a kind" so dear to Mr. Webb.

This trend is far too significant to be dismissed—along with organic gardens and communes—as nothing but a stale leftover from the Sixties[1]. True, people who are moving from city to country are younger—by about seventeen years—than those who are staying put[2]; but statistics also show that they earn about $1,500 more annually, they have higher-status jobs, and they have on the average two years more education than their cohorts who have chosen to remain in urban areas. Nor are movers simply spilling over from city to suburb: People are heading for small towns that are independent of cities. Although some of these areas are within commuting distance of cities and suburbs, the most spectacular growth is taking place in towns far from urban centers.

What is most important about this trend, however, is not so much the types of people and towns involved as the fact that the shift represents an abrupt and dramatic break with the American tradition of urban expansion. For an entire century, people have abandoned the rustic amenities of country living in favor of urban sophistication and convenience. By the Sixties, city life seemed so important to our culture that the President's Commission on Rural Poverty called its report "The People Left Behind." Indeed they were: Some two hundred counties had lost more than half their population to cities, and hundreds of others had dwindled almost as dramatically.

In the sociological literature, country folk have seemed not so much "the people left behind" as the people entirely forgotten—as evidenced by the titles that line library shelves: *The Urbanization of America; The Making of Urban America*; *The Urban Prospect.* Even Robert and Helen Lynd's classic *Middletown* (1929) and *Middletown in Transition* (1937)—both recognized as being

1. 1960년대
2. to remain in one place; not move

among the most valuable records on an American community ever written—deal not with a small town but with a small city—Muncie, Indiana, thinly disguised. During the ten years in which the Lynds scrutinized "Middletown," its population grew from 36,000 to 50,000.

But even though the Lynds dealt with a middling-big[3] town, they said a lot about small ones in between the lines. In *Middletown*, rural America slowly became an anachronism as the town began to pulse with life, thanks to a natural gas boom and the advent of the auto and radio. Then in *Transition* the Lynds began to note the many admirable qualities of life Middletown's people had sacrificed in their rush to urbanization. "'Progress'; 'growing' wealth and power; 'bigger and better' everything—these are some of the symbols that live daily in the skins of Middletown folk," the Lynds wrote. "People tend to lose each other....One 'lives in' a town, 'makes one's money there,'...rather than necessarily being an integral part of the town."

Despite the isolation that characterized city life, however, decades passed and the small-town exodus and concurrent urban explosion continued. People examined their options and chose to buck cosmopolitan problems rather than wrestle with rural ones.

The choice was not altogether irrational. The problems that plague small towns remain serious even today. Health facilities are the worst of the lot: In 1970 there were half as many doctors per 100,000 people in nonmetropolitan areas as there were in metropolitan areas. Chronic disease and infant mortality have far higher incidence in small towns, and old people who live in them have so many health problems—and find it so difficult to reach a doctor—that life for many of them ranges

---

3. between large and small, good and bad, etc.,

from the unpleasant to the unbearable.

Income is another problem. Nonmetropolitan residents earn only three fourths as much as city dwellers, and the difference is not wholly made up, as one might expect, in the lower cost of living. Worse, jobs are scarce: Should a factory close down outside a small town, there isn't another one a few blocks away to soak up the unemployed. Twice as many of the nation's poor live in nonmetropolitan areas as in cities. Finally, people who live in rural areas are less educated, and their attitudes are often very fundamental and conservative—partly because, sociologists say, they don't have the city dweller's exposure to many different ideas. As a result, small-town people may appear naive or narrow-minded to city dwellers who are considering a move to the country.

Why then, with all the problems and after all these years, are so many city people now moving to small towns? Some reasons are obvious: Industries and businesses are moving to small towns, so more jobs are available. Better communications and transportation make for easier access to the city's benefits. The crime rates in cities have soared to such heights that many people are simply afraid to stay; the incidence of aggressive assault is twice as high in cities as in small towns, and the rate of robberies is thirteen times as high. Another factor is pollution. Too many cities have taken shortcuts in their race to profits, refusing to spend the money necessary to make their products or produce their energy in a safe, clean way. The environmental mess is no longer just a rallying point for people who are enamored of causes; statistics show that many of the people who are fleeing cities have lung and heart diseases caused by pollution and are too sick to take any more chances.

Sociological theories tell us more about the move to small towns than do any of the random factual or statistical explanations. In an article published in *The Geographical Review,* Wilbur Zelinsky hypothesizes that the more progressive a society becomes, the less the people flock toward traditional symbols of progress. As a society advances, he writes, economic features are not as important to them as human values, pleasures, and physical surroundings.

Another theory about the country's magnetic pull is developed with elaborate detail and admirable expertise in an issue of *The Annals of the American Academy* devoted to the "New Rural America" (January 1977). The numerous sociologists who contributed to this issue suggest that Americans have never wanted to live in the city at all; that the economic factor did not influence their choice—it *forced* their choice. Now that many Americans have achieved financial well-being, the *Annals* symposium suggests, they are concentrating on other needs—and are fulfilling these needs by moving to small towns. This theory is supported by Angus Campbell, whose studies show that although urban dwellers are satisfied with the specifics of life—hospitals, garbage collection, and so forth—they usually are not happy about life in toto[4]. Rural people, on the other hand, are satisfied more with the whole of their life than with any of its parts. Another telling statistic from the *Annals* report: Six out of ten city dwellers want to move from the metropolitan areas; but nine out of ten small-town people wouldn't trade their life for any other.

Because the urban exodus of recent years began so suddenly, the sociological analysis of small-town living is currently more an art than a science. Besides examining the changing attitudes and values of Americans, sociologists have yet to address themselves

---

4. (L) totally; as a whole

to other pressing questions raised by the new preference for small towns: How can they avoid the problems that plague the cities? How, for instance, can they cope with the population influx? Who should assume the high cost of providing services for rural areas? Few minorities move to small towns; how can villages avoid being characterized as racially and socially exclusive?

Social scientists will, for some time to come, be writing and publishing furiously on these topics. In the meantime, the Americans who have left the urban rat race and settled down in the countryside can finally concentrate, not on earning a living, but on savoring life itself.

STAGE MANAGER: "And this is Mrs. Webb's garden. Just like Mrs. Gibbs's, only it's got a lot of sunflowers, too. Right here's a big butternut tree..." He looks at the audience for a minute. "Nice town, y'know what I mean?"

EXERCISES

A. *Answer the following questions.*

1. Why are major cities losing population to small towns?
2. Do you think more and more people will be moving from city to country in the future?
3. Do you agree with the author's assessments of the urban and rural life?
4. What other factors can you think of that might influence the migration from city to country?
5. Where would people choose to live if salary and expenses were equal?

B. *Write in each blank space a word that fits naturally.*

1. For the first time in fifty years, more Americans are moving to small towns than to (   ).
2. In three short years after 1970, 1.5 million left metropolitan areas behind and headed for homes in (   ) towns.
3. People who are moving from city to (   ) are younger than those who are staying put.
4. Although some of these areas are (   ) commuting distance of cities and suburbs, the most spectacular growth is taking place in towns far from urban centers.
5. People are heading for small towns that are independent (   ) cities.
6. It is not so (   ) the types of people and towns involved as the fact that the shift represents an abrupt and dramatic break.
7. Why then, (   ) all the problems and after all these years, are so many city people now moving to small towns?
8. Better communications and transportation make for easier access (   ) the city's benefits.
9. The crime rates in cities have soared to (   ) heights that many people are simply afraid to stay.
10. Nine out of ten small-town people wouldn't trade their life (   ) any other.
11. The studies show that although urban dwellers are satisfied with the specifics of life—hospitals, garbage collection, and (   ) forth—they usually are not happy about life in toto.

C. *Choose one of the words that best fits each of the following sentences.*

a. stale　b. exclusive　c. urbanization　d. conservative
e. exodus　f. expansion　g. pollution　h. anachronism
i. cohorts　j. amenities　k. allure

1. Few minorities move to small towns; how can villages avoid being characterized as racially and socially (　　　)?
2. Many of the people who are fleeing cities have lung and heart diseases caused by (　　　).
3. The once magical attractions of cosmopolitan life no longer have the (　　　) of those simple country "pleasures of a kind".
4. This trend is far too significant to be dismissed as nothing but a (　　　) leftover from the Sixties.
5. They have on the average two years more education than their (　　　) who have chosen to remain in urban areas.
6. The shift represents an abrupt and dramatic break with the American tradition of urban (　　　).
7. People have abandoned the rustic (　　　) of country living in favor of urban sophistication and convenience.
8. Rural America slowly became an (　　　) as the town began to pulse with life, thanks to a natural gas boom and the advent of the auto.
9. They began to note the many admirable qualities of life the people had sacrificed in their rush to (　　　).
10. Despite the isolation that characterized city life, decades passed and the small-town (　　　) and concurrent urban explosion continued.
11. People who live in rural areas are less educated, and their attitudes are often very fundamental and (　　　).

14. Fifth Avenue Uptown

A Letter from Harlem

JAMES BALDWIN*

There is a housing project standing now where the house in which we grew up once stood, and one of those stunted city trees is snarling where our doorway used to be. This is on the rehabilitated side of the avenue. The other side of the avenue—for progress takes time—has not been rehabilitated yet and it looks exactly as it looked in the days when we sat with our noses pressed against the windowpane, longing to be allowed to go "across the street." The grocery store which gave us credit is still there, and there can be no doubt that it is still giving credit. The people in the project certainly need it—far more, indeed, than they ever needed the project. The last time I passed by, the Jewish proprietor was still standing among his shelves, looking sadder and heavier but scarcely any older. Farther down the block stands the shoe-repair store in which our shoes were repaired until reparation became impossible and in which, then, we bought all our "new" ones. The Negro proprietor is still in the window, head down,

---

* **James Baldwin(1924～1987):** 미국의 소설가, 수필가, 극작가. 9남매 중 장남으로 Harlem에서 출생. 뒤에 잡역부, 급사, 공원으로 일하며 밤에는 글을 씀. 저서로는 Go Tell It on the Mountain(1952), Nobody Knows My Name(1961)등이 있음

working at the leather.

These two, I imagine, could tell a long tale if they would (perhaps they would be glad to if they could), having watched so many, for so long, struggling in the fishhooks, the barbed wire, of this avenue.

The avenue is elsewhere the renowned and elegant Fifth. The area I am describing, which, in today's gang parlance, would be called "the turf[1]," is bounded by Lenox Avenue on the west, the Harlem River on the east, 135th Street on the north, and 130th Street on the south. We never lived beyond these boundaries; this is where we grew up. Walking along 145th Street—for example—familiar as it is, and similar, does not have the same impact because I do not know any of the people on the block. But when I turn east on 131st Street and Lenox Avenue, there is first a soda-pop joint, then a shoeshine "parlor," then a grocery store, then a dry cleaners', then the houses. All along the street there are people who watched me grow up, people who grew up with me, people I watched grow up along with my brothers and sisters; and sometimes in my arms, sometimes underfoot, sometimes at my shoulder—or on it—their children, a riot, a forest of children, who include my nieces and nephews.

When we reach the end of this long block, we find ourselves on wide, filthy, hostile Fifth Avenue, facing that project which hangs over the avenue like a monument to the folly, and the cowardice, of good intentions. All along the block, for anyone who knows it, are immense human gaps, like craters. These gaps are not created merely by those who have moved away, inevitably

1. (slang) an area claimed by a group as its own (especially by young gang members)

into some other ghetto; or by those who have risen, almost always into a greater capacity for self-loathing and self-delusion; or yet by those who, by whatever means—World War II, the Korean war, a policeman's gun or billy, a gang war, a brawl, madness, an overdose of heroin, or, simply, unnatural exhaustion—are dead. I am talking about those who are left, and I am talking principally about the young. What are they doing? Well, some, a minority, are fanatical churchgoers, members of the more extreme of the Holy Roller sects. Many, many more are "Moslems," by affiliation or sympathy, that is to say that they are united by nothing more—and nothing less—than a hatred of the white world and all its works. They are present, for example, at every Buy Black[2] street-corner meeting—meetings in which the speaker urges his hearers to cease trading with white men and establish a separate economy. Neither the speaker nor his hearers can possibly do this, of course, since Negroes do not own General Motors or RCA[3] or the A & P[4], nor, indeed, do they own more than a wholly insufficient fraction of anything else in Harlem (those who *do* own anything are more interested in their profits than in their fellows). But these meetings nevertheless keep alive in the participators a certain pride of bitterness without which, however futile this bitterness may be, they could scarcely remain alive at all. Many have given up. They stay home and watch the TV screen, living on the earnings of their parents, cousins, brothers, or uncles, and only leave the house to go to the movies or to the nearest bar. "How're you making it?[5]" one may ask, running

2. 흑인들 가게의 물건을 사주자는
3. the Radio Corporation of America, 미국의 거대한 음향기기 회사
4. Great Atlantic and Pacific Tea Company, 미국의 거대한 수퍼마킷 이름
5. 잘해 내다, 여기서는 잘 지내다

into them along the block, or in the bar. "Oh, I'm TV-ing it"; with the saddest, sweetest, most shamefaced of smiles, and from a great distance. This distance one is compelled to respect; anyone who has traveled so far will not easily be dragged again into the world. There are further retreats, of course, than the TV screen or the bar. There are those who are simply sitting on their stoops, "stoned[6]," animated for a moment only, and hideously, by the approach of someone who may lend them the money for a "fix[7]." Or by the approach of someone from whom they can purchase it, one of the shrewd ones, on the way to prison or just coming out.

And the others, who have avoided all of these deaths, get up in the morning and go downtown to meet "the man[8]." They work in the white man's world all day and come home in the evening to this fetid block. They struggle to instill in their children some private sense of honor or dignity which will help the child to survive. This means, of course, that they must struggle, stolidly, incessantly, to keep this sense alive in themselves, in spite of the insults, the indifference, and the cruelty they are certain to encounter in their working day. They patiently browbeat the landlord into fixing the heat, the plaster, the plumbing; this demands prodigious patience; nor is patience usually enough. In trying to make their hovels habitable, they are perpetually throwing good money after bad. Such frustration, so long endured, is driving many strong, admirable men and women whose only crime is color to the very gates of paranoia.

One remembers them from another time—playing handball in

---

6. (slang) very drunk
7. (slang) 마약 주사
8. (slang) 백인, 경찰관

the playground, going to church, wondering if they were going to be promoted at school. One remembers them going off to war—gladly, to escape this block. One remembers their return. Perhaps one remembers their wedding day. And one sees where the girl is now—vainly looking for salvation from some other embittered, trussed, and struggling boy—and sees the all-but-abandoned children in the streets.

Now I am perfectly aware that there are other slums in which white men are fighting for their lives, and mainly losing. I know that blood is also flowing through those streets and that the human damage there is incalculable. People are continually pointing out to me the wretchedness of white people in order to console me for the wretchedness of blacks. But an itemized account of the American failure does not console me and it should not console anyone else. That hundreds of thousands of white people are living, in effect, no better than the "niggers" is not a fact to be regarded with complacency. The social and moral bankruptcy suggested by this fact is of the bitterest, most terrifying kind.

The people, however, who believe that this democratic anguish has some consoling value are always pointing out that So-and-So, white, and So-and-So, black, rose from the slums into the big time[9]. The existence—the public existence—of, say, Frank Sinatra and Sammy Davis, Jr., proves to them that America is still the land of opportunity and that inequalities vanish before the determined will. It proves nothing of the sort. The determined will is rare—at the moment, in this country, it is unspeakably rare—and the inequalities suffered by the many are in no way justified by the rise of a few. A few have always risen—in every

9. 제일급의

country, every era, and in the teeth of[10] regimes which can by no stretch of the imagination[11] be thought of as free. Not all of these people, it is worth remembering, left the world better than they found it. The determined will is rare, but it is not invariably benevolent. Furthermore, the American equation of success with the big time reveals an awful disrespect for human life and human achievement. This equation has placed our cities among the most dangerous in the world and has placed our youth among the most empty and most bewildered. The situation of our youth is not mysterious. Children have never been very good at listening to their elders, but they have never failed to imitate them. They must, they have no other models. That is exactly what our children are doing. They are imitating our immorality, our disrespect for the pain of others.

All other slum dwellers, when the bank account permits it, can move out of the slum and vanish altogether from the eye of persecution. No Negro in this country has ever made that much money and it will be a long time before any Negro does. The Negroes in Harlem, who have no money, spend what they have on such gimcracks as they are sold. These include "wider" TV screens, more "faithful" hi-fi sets, more "powerful" cars, all of which, of course, are obsolete long before they are paid for. Anyone who has ever struggled with poverty knows how extremely expensive it is to be poor; and if one is a member of a captive population, economically speaking, one's feet have simply been placed on the treadmill forever. One is victimized, economically, in a thousand ways—rent, for example, or car insurance. Go shopping one day in Harlem—for anything—and

10. in spite of opposition, 무릅쓰고
11. 제멋대로 상상하여도

compare Harlem prices and quality with those downtown.

The people who have managed to get off this block have only got as far as a more respectable ghetto. This respectable ghetto does not even have the advantages of the disreputable one—friends, neighbors, a familiar church, and friendly tradesmen; and it is not, moreover, in the nature of any ghetto to remain respectable long. Every Sunday, people who have left the block take the lonely ride back, dragging their increasingly discontented children with them. They spend the day talking, not always with words, about the trouble they've seen and the trouble—one must watch their eyes as they watch their children—they are only too likely to see. For children do not like ghettos. It takes them nearly no time to discover exactly why they are there.

The projects in Harlem are hated. They are hated almost as much as policemen, and this is saying a great deal. And they are hated for the same reason: both reveal, unbearably, the real attitude of the white world, no matter how many liberal speeches are made, no matter how many lofty editorials are written, no matter how many civil-rights commissions are set up.

The projects are hideous, of course, there being a law, apparently respected throughout the world, that popular housing shall be as cheerless as prison. They are lumped all over Harlem, colorless, bleak, high, and revolting. The wide windows look out on Harlem's invincible and indescribable squalor: the Park Avenue railroad tracks, around which, about forty years ago, the present dark community began; the unrehabilitated houses, bowed down, it would seem, under the great weight of frustration and bitterness they contain; the dark, the ominous schoolhouses from which the child may emerge maimed, blinded, hooked, or enraged for life; and the churches, churches, block upon block of churches, niched in the walls like cannon in the walls of a fortress. Even if the administration of the projects were not so insanely humiliating (for example: one must report raises in salary to the management, which will then eat up the profit by raising one's rent; the management has the right to know who is staying in your apartment; the management can ask you to leave, at their discretion), the projects would still be hated because they are an insult to the meanest intelligence.

Harlem got its first private project, Riverton—which is now, naturally, a slum—about twelve years ago because at that time Negroes were not allowed to live in Stuyvesant Town. Harlem watched Riverton go up, therefore, in the most violent bitterness of spirit, and hated it long before the builders arrived. They began hating it at about the time people began moving out of their condemned houses to make room for this additional proof of how thoroughly the white world despised them. And they had scarcely moved in, naturally, before they began smashing windows, defacing walls, urinating in the elevators, and fornicating in the playgrounds. Liberals, both white and black, were appalled at the spectacle. I was appalled by the liberal innocence—or cynicism, which comes out in practice as much the same thing. Other people were delighted to be able to point to proof positive that nothing could be done to better the lot of the colored people. They were, and are, right in one respect: that nothing can be done as long as they are treated like colored people. The people in Harlem know they are living there because white people do not think they are good enough to live anywhere else. No amount of "improvement" can sweeten this fact. Whatever money is now being earmarked to improve this, or any other ghetto, might as well be burnt. A ghetto can be improved in one way only: out of existence.

Similarly, the only way to police a ghetto is to be oppressive. None of the Police Commissioner's men, even with the best will in the world, have any way of understanding the lives led by the people they swagger about in twos and threes controlling. Their very presence is an insult, and it would be, even if they spent their entire day feeding gumdrops to children. They represent the force of the white world, and that world's real intentions are, simply, for that world's criminal profit and ease, to keep the black man corralled up here, in his place. The badge, the gun in the holster, and the swinging club make vivid what will happen should his rebellion become overt. Rare, indeed, is the Harlem citizen, from the most circumspect church member to the most shiftless adolescent, who does not have a long tale to tell of police incompetence, injustice, or brutality. I myself have witnessed and endured it more than once. The businessmen and racketeers also have a story. And so do the prostitutes. (And this is not, perhaps, the place to discuss Harlem's very complex attitude toward black policemen, nor the reasons, according to Harlem, that they are nearly all downtown.)

It is hard, on the other hand, to blame the policeman, blank, good-natured, thoughtless, and insuperably innocent, for being such a perfect representative of the people he serves. He, too, believes in good intentions and is astounded and offended when they are not taken for the deed. He has never, himself, done anything for which to be hated—which of us has? —and yet he is facing, daily and nightly, people who would gladly see him dead, and he knows it. There is no way for him not to know it: there are few things under heaven more unnerving than the silent, accumulating contempt and hatred of a people. He moves through Harlem, therefore, like an occupying soldier in a bitterly hostile country; which is precisely what, and where, he is, and is the reason he walks in twos and threes. And he is not the only one who knows why he is always in company: the people who are watching him know why, too. Any street meeting, sacred or secular, which he and his colleagues uneasily cover has as its explicit or implicit burden the cruelty and injustice of the white domination. And these days, of course, in terms increasingly vivid and jubilant, it speaks of the end of that domination. The white policeman standing on a Harlem street corner finds himself at the very center of the revolution now occurring in the world. He is not prepared for it—naturally, nobody is—and, what is possibly much more to the point, he is exposed, as few white people are, to the anguish of the black people around him. Even if he is gifted with the merest mustard grain of imagination, something must seep in. He cannot avoid observing that some of the children, in spite of their color, remind him of children he has known and loved, perhaps even of his own children. He knows that he certainly does not want *his* children living this way. He can retreat from his uneasiness in only one direction: into a callousness which very shortly becomes second nature. He becomes more callous, the population becomes more hostile, the situation grows more tense, and the police force is increased. One day, to everyone's astonishment, someone drops a match in the powder keg and everything blows up. Before the dust has settled or the blood congealed, editorials, speeches, and civil-rights commissions are loud in the land demanding to know what happened. What happened is that Negroes want to be treated like men.

Negroes want to be treated like men: a perfectly straightforward statement, containing only seven words. People who have mastered Kant, Hegel, Shakespeare, Marx, Freud, and the Bible find this statement utterly impenetrable. The idea seems to threaten profound, barely conscious assumptions. A kind of panic paralyzes their features, as though they found themselves trapped on the edge of a steep place. I once tried to describe to a very well-known American intellectual the conditions among Negroes in the South. My recital disturbed him and made him indignant; and he asked me in perfect innocence, "Why don't all the Negroes in the South move North?" I tried to explain what *has* happened, unfailingly, whenever a significant body of Negroes move North. They do not escape Jim Crow[12]: they merely encounter another, not-less-deadly variety. They do not move to Chicago, they move to the South Side; they do not move to New York, they move to Harlem. The pressure within the ghetto causes the ghetto walls to expand, and this expansion is always violent. White people hold the line as long as they can, and in as many ways as they can, from verbal intimidation to physical violence. But inevitably the border which has divided the ghetto from the rest of the world falls into the hands of the ghetto. The white people fall back bitterly before the black horde; the landlords make a tidy profit by raising the rent, chopping up the rooms, and all but dispensing with the upkeep; and what has once been a neighborhood turns into a "turf." This is precisely what happened when the Puerto Ricans arrived in their thousands—and the bitterness thus caused is, as I write, being fought out all up and down those streets.

Northerners indulge in an extremely dangerous luxury. They seem to feel that because they fought on the right side during the Civil War, and won, they have earned the right merely to deplore what is going on in the South, without taking any responsibility for it; and that they can ignore what is happening in Northern cities

12. 흑인 차별정책

because what is happening in Little Rock[13] or Birmingham[14] is worse. Well, in the first place, it is not possible for anyone who has not endured both to know which is "worse." I know Negroes who prefer the South and white Southerners, because "At least there, you haven't got to play any guessing games!" The guessing games referred to have driven more than one Negro into the narcotics ward, the madhouse, or the river. I know another Negro, a man very dear to me, who says, with conviction and with truth, "The spirit of the South is the spirit of America." He was born in the North and did his military training in the South. He did not, as far as I can gather, find the South "worse"; he found it, if anything, all too familiar. In the second place, though, even if Birmingham is worse, no doubt Johannesburg, South Africa, beats it by several miles, and Buchenwald[15] was one of the worst things that ever happened in the entire history of the world. The world has never lacked for horrifying examples; but I do not believe that these examples are meant to be used as justification for our own crimes. This perpetual justification empties the heart of all human feeling. The emptier our hearts become, the greater will be our crimes. Thirdly, the South is not merely an embarrassingly backward region, but a part of this country, and what happens there concerns every one of us.

As far as the color problem is concerned, there is but one great difference between the Southern white and the Northerner: the Southerner remembers, historically and in his own psyche, a kind of Eden in which he loved black people and they loved him. Historically, the flaming sword laid across this Eden is the Civil

---

13. the capital of the US state of Arkansas
14. a city in Alabama in the US
15. a concentration camp near Weimar in SW Germany during the Second World War

War. Personally, it is the Southerner's sexual coming of age, when, without any warning, unbreakable taboos are set up between himself and his past. Everything, thereafter, is permitted him except the love he remembers and has never ceased to need. The resulting, indescribable torment affects every Southern mind and is the basis of the Southern hysteria.

None of this is true for the Northerner. Negroes represent nothing to him personally, except, perhaps, the dangers of carnality. He never sees Negroes. Southerners see them all the time. Northerners never think about them whereas Southerners are never really thinking of anything else. Negroes are, therefore, ignored in the North and are under surveillance in the South, and suffer hideously in both places. Neither the Southerner nor the Northerner is able to look on the Negro simply as a man. It seems to be indispensable to the national self-esteem that the Negro be considered either as a kind of ward (in which case we are told how many Negroes, comparatively, bought Cadillacs last year and how few, comparatively, were lynched), or as a victim (in which case we are promised that he will never vote in our assemblies or go to school with our kids). They are two sides of the same coin and the South will not change—*cannot* change—until the North changes. The country will not change until it reexamines itself and discovers what it really means by freedom. In the meantime, generations keep being born, bitterness is increased by incompetence, pride, and folly, and the world shrinks around us.

It is a terrible, an inexorable, law that one cannot deny the humanity of another without diminishing one's own: in the face of one's victim, one sees oneself. Walk through the streets of Harlem and see what we, this nation, have become.

EXERCISES

A. *Answer the following questions.*

1. What images does the writer try to give with "Fifth Avenue Uptown"?
2. What do fishhooks and barbed wire symbolize?
3. What does the writer mean by immense human gaps along the block?
4. What is the purpose of this essay?
5. Is he objective in depicting the situation in Harlem?

B. *Give the correct forms of the words given in the brackets.*

1. The other side of the avenue looks exactly as it looked in the days when we sat with our noses (press) against the windowpane, (long) to be allowed to go "across the street."
2. Such frustration, so long (endurance), is driving many strong, admirable men and women whose only crime is color to the very gates of paranoia.
3. They are imitating our immorality, our (respect) for the pain of others.
4. None of the policemen have any way of understanding the lives led by the people they swagger about in twos and threes (control).
5. People who have mastered Kant, Hegel, Shakespeare, Marx, Freud, and the Bible find this statement utterly (penetrate).

C. *Fill in the blanks with suitable words.*

1. They patiently browbeat the landlord (   ) fixing the heat, the plaster, the plumbing; this demands prodigious patience;

nor is patience usually enough.

2. In trying to make their hovels habitable, they are perpetually throwing good money ( ) bad.
3. The American equation of success ( ) the big time reveals an awful disrespect for human life and human achievement.
4. Anyone who has ever struggled with poverty knows how extremely expensive ( ) is to be poor.
5. And they had scarcely moved in, naturally, ( ) they began smashing windows.
6. The badge, the gun in the holster, and the swinging club make vivid what will happen ( ) his rebellion become overt.
7. Any street meeting, sacred or secular, which he and his colleagues uneasily cover has as its explicit or ( ) burden the cruelty and injustice of the white domination.
8. This perpetual justification empties the heart ( ) all human feeling.
9. The country will not change until it reexamines itself and discovers what it really means ( ) freedom.
10. It is a terrible, an inexorable, law that one cannot deny the humanity of another ( ) diminishing one's own.

It is said that for money you can have everything, but you cannot; You can buy food, but not appetite; medicine, but not health; knowledge, but not wisdom; glitter, but not beauty; fun, but not joy; acquaintances, but not friends; servants, but not loyalty; leisure, but not peace. You can have the husk of everything for money, but not the kernel.

Arne Garborg

15. The Spider and the Wasp

ALEXANDER PETRUNKEVITCH*

In the feeding and safeguarding of their progeny[1] insects and spiders exhibit some interesting analogies to reasoning and some crass examples of blind instinct. The case I propose to describe here is that of the tarantula spiders and their archenemy, the digger wasps of the genus Pepsis. It is a classic example of what looks like intelligence pitted against[2] instinct—a strange situation in which the victim, though fully able to defend itself, submits unwittingly to its destruction.

Most tarantulas live in the tropics, but several species occur in the temperate zone and a few are common in the southern United States. Some varieties are large and have powerful fangs with which they can inflict a deep wound. These formidable looking spiders do not, however, attack man; you can hold one in your hand, if you are gentle, without being bitten. Their bite is dangerous only to insects and small mammals such as mice; for a man it is no worse than a hornet's sting.

---

* **Alexander Petrunkevitch (1875～1964):** Ukraine 태생의 동물학자로서 Moscow와 독일에서 공부를 마치고 미국의 Harvard大, Yale大등의 대학에서 동물학을 강의했으며 An Inquiry into the Natural Classification of Spiders(1933), A Study of Paleozoic Arachnida(1964)등의 저서가 있음

1. 후손
2. set into opposition or rivalry

Tarantulas customarily live in deep cylindrical burrows, from which they emerge at dusk and into which they retire at dawn. Mature males wander about after dark in search of females and occasionally stray into houses. After mating, the male dies in a few weeks, but a female lives much longer and can mate several years in succession. In a Paris museum is a tropical specimen which is said to have been living in captivity for 25 years.

A fertilized female tarantula lays from 200 to 400 eggs at a time; thus it is possible for a single tarantula to produce several thousand young. She takes no care of them beyond weaving a cocoon of silk to enclose the eggs. After they hatch, the young walk away, find convenient places in which to dig their burrows and spend the rest of their lives in solitude. The eyesight of tarantulas is poor, being limited to a sensing of change in the intensity of light and to the perception of moving objects. They apparently have little or no sense of hearing, for a hungry tarantula will pay no attention to a loudly chirping cricket placed in its cage unless the insect happens to touch one of its legs.

But all spiders, and especially hairy ones, have an extremely delicate sense of touch. Laboratory experiments prove that tarantulas can distinguish three types of touch: pressure against the body wall, stroking of the body hair, and riffling of certain very fine hairs on the legs called trichobothria. Pressure against the body, by a finger or the end of a pencil, causes the tarantula to move off slowly for a short distance. The touch excites no defensive response unless the approach is from above where the spider can see the motion, in which case it rises on its hind legs, lifts its front legs, opens its fangs and holds this threatening posture as long as the object continues to move.

The entire body of a tarantula, especially its legs, is thickly clothed with hair. Some of it is short and woolly, some long and stiff. Touching this body hair produces one of two distinct reactions. When the spider is hungry, it responds with an immediate and swift attack. At the touch of a cricket's antennae the tarantula seizes the insect so swiftly that a motion picture taken at the rate of 64 frames per second shows only the result and not the process of capture. But when the spider is not hungry, the stimulation of its hairs merely causes it to shake the touched limb. An insect can walk under its hairy belly unharmed.

The trichobothria, very fine hairs growing from disklike membranes on the legs, are sensitive only to air movement. A light breeze makes them vibrate slowly without disturbing the common hair. When one blows gently on the trichobothria, the tarantula reacts with a quick jerk of its four front legs. If the front and hind legs are stimulated at the same time, the spider makes a sudden jump. This reaction is quite independent of the state of its appetite.

These three tactile responses—to pressure on the body wall, to moving of the common hair and to flexing of the trichobothria—are so different from one another that there is no possibility of confusing them. They serve the tarantula adequately for most of its needs and enable it to avoid most annoyances and dangers. But they fail the spider completely when it meets its deadly enemy, the digger wasp Pepsis.

These solitary wasps are beautiful and formidable creatures. Most species are either a deep shiny blue all over, or deep blue with rusty wings. The largest have a wing span of about four inches. They live on nectar. When excited, they give off a pungent odor—a warning that they are ready to attack. The sting is much worse than that of a bee or common wasp, and the pain and swelling last longer. In the adult stage, the wasp lives only a few months. The female produces but a few eggs, one at a time at intervals of two or three days. For each egg the mother must provide one adult tarantula, alive but paralyzed. The mother wasp attaches the egg to the paralyzed spider's abdomen. Upon hatching from the egg, the larva is many hundreds of times smaller than its living but helpless victim. It eats no other food and drinks no water. By the time it has finished its single gargantuan[3] meal and become ready for wasphood, nothing remains of the tarantula but its indigestible chitinous skeleton.

The mother wasp goes tarantula-hunting when the egg in her ovary is almost ready to be laid. Flying low over the ground late on a sunny afternoon, the wasp looks for its victim or for the mouth of a tarantula burrow, a round hole edged by a bit of silk. The sex of the spider makes no difference, but the mother is highly discriminating as to species. Each species of Pepsis requires a certain species of tarantula, and the wasp will not attack the wrong species. In a cage with a tarantula which is not its normal prey, the wasp avoids the spider and is usually killed by it in the night.

Yet when a wasp finds the correct species, it is the other way about[4]. To identify the species, the wasp apparently must explore the spider with her antennae. The tarantula shows an amazing tolerance to this exploration. The wasp crawls under it and walks over it without evoking any hostile response. The molestation is so great and so persistent that the tarantula often rises on all eight legs, as if it were on stilts. It may stand this way for several minutes. Meanwhile the wasp, having satisfied itself that the

3. 거대한
4. 거꾸로, 반대로

victim is of the right species, moves off a few inches to dig the spider's grave. Working vigorously with legs and jaws, it excavates a hole 8 to 10 inches deep with a diameter slightly larger than the spider's girth. Now and again, the wasp pops out of the hole to make sure that the spider is still there.

When the grave is finished, the wasp returns to the tarantula to complete her ghastly enterprise. First she feels it all over once more with her antennae. Then her behavior becomes more aggressive. She bends her abdomen, protruding her sting, and searches for the soft membrane at the point where the spider's legs join its body—the only spot where she can penetrate the horny skeleton. From time to time, as the exasperated spider slowly shifts ground, the wasp turns on her back and slides along with the aid of her wings, trying to get under the tarantula for a shot at the vital spot. During all this maneuvering, which can last for several minutes, the tarantula makes no move to save itself. Finally the wasp corners it against some obstruction and grasps one of its legs in her powerful jaws. Now at last the harassed spider tries a desperate but vain defense. The two contestants roll over and over on the ground. It is a terrifying sight, and the outcome is always the same. The wasp finally manages to thrust her sting into the soft spot and holds it there for a few seconds while she pumps in the poison. Almost immediately the tarantula falls paralyzed on its back. Its legs stop twitching; its heart stops beating. Yet it is not dead, as is shown by the fact that if taken from the wasp it can be restored to some sensitivity by being kept in a moist chamber for several months.

After paralyzing the tarantula, the wasp cleans herself by dragging her body along the ground and rubbing her feet, sucks the drop of blood oozing from the wound in the spider's abdomen, then grabs a leg of the flabby, helpless animal in her jaws and drags it down to the bottom of the grave. She stays there for many minutes, sometimes for several hours, and what she does all that time in the dark we do not know. Eventually she lays her egg and attaches it to the side of the spider's abdomen with a sticky secretion. Then she emerges, fills the grave with soil carried bit by bit in her jaws, and finally tramples the ground all around to hide any trace of the grave from prowlers. Then she flies away, leaving her descendant safely started in life.

In all this the behavior of the wasp evidently is qualitatively different from that of the spider. The wasp acts like an intelligent animal. This is not to say that instinct plays no part or that she reasons as man does. But her actions are to the point[5] ; they are not automatic and can be modified to fit the situation. We do not know for certain how she identifies the tarantula—probably it is by some olfactory[6] or chemo-tactile sense—but she does it purposefully and does not blindly tackle a wrong species.

On the other hand, the tarantula's behavior shows only confusion. Evidently the wasp's pawing gives it no pleasure, for it tries to move away. That the wasp is not simulating sexual stimulation is certain, because male and female tarantulas react in the same way to its advances. That the spider is not anesthetized by some odorless secretion is easily shown by blowing lightly at the tarantula and making it jump suddenly. What, then, makes the tarantula behave as stupidly as it does?

No clear, simple answer is available. Possibly the stimulation by the wasp's antennae is masked by a heavier pressure on the spider's

---

5. 적절한, 요령있는
6. 후각의

body, so that it reacts as when prodded by a pencil. But the explanation may be much more complex. Initiative in attack is not in the nature of tarantulas; most species fight only when cornered so that escape is impossible. Their inherited patterns of behavior apparently prompt them to avoid problems rather than attack them. For example, spiders always weave their webs in three dimensions, and when a spider finds that there is insufficient space to attach certain threads in the third dimension, it leaves the place and seeks another, instead of finishing the web in a single plane. This urge to escape seems to arise under all circumstances, in all phases of life, and to take the place of reasoning. For a spider to change the pattern of its web is as impossible as for an inexperienced man to build a bridge across a chasm obstructing his way.

In a way, the instinctive urge to escape is not only easier but often more efficient than reasoning. The tarantula does exactly what is most efficient in all cases except in an encounter with a ruthless and determined attacker dependent for the existence of her own species on killing as many tarantulas as she can lay eggs. Perhaps in this case the spider follows its usual pattern of trying to escape, instead of seizing and killing the wasp, because it is not aware of its danger. In any case, the survival of the tarantula species as a whole is protected by the fact that the spider is much more fertile than the wasp.

Happiness is not the goal of our lives but the consequences of how we live. Happiness is like our shadow: it runs away when we chase after it, but when we walk toward the sunlight and truth, it follows us. Dario Lostado

EXERCISES

A. *Answer the following questions.*

1. In what ways does the wasp seem rational?
2. In what ways does the spider seem irrational?
3. What kind of people resemble Pepsis wasps?
4. What kind of people resemble tarantulas?
5. What qualities in the author's writing make his essay so interesting to read?

B. *Give the correct forms of the words given in the brackets.*

1. You can hold one in your hand, if you are gentle, without (bite).
2. Some of it is short and (wool), some long and stiff.
3. An insect can walk under its hairy belly (harm).
4. When (excite), they give off a pungent odor—a warning that they are ready to attack.
5. For each egg the mother must provide one adult tarantula, alive but (paralyze).
6. The wasp looks for its victim or for the mouth of a tarantula burrow, a round hole(edge) by a bit of silk.
7. Yet it is not dead, as is shown by the fact that if (take) from the wasp it can be restored to some sensitivity.
8. Then she flies away, leaving her descendant safely (start) in life.
9. A hungry tarantula pays no attention to a loudly chirping cricket (place) in its cage unless the insect happens to touch one of its legs.

C. *Fill in the blanks with suitable words.*

1. Insects and spiders exhibit some interesting analogies ( ) reasoning and some crass examples of blind instinct.
2. It is a classic example of ( ) looks like intelligence pitted against instinct.
3. Mature males wander about after dark in search ( ) females and occasionally stray into houses.
4. But a female lives much longer and can mate several years ( ) succession.
5. In a Paris museum is a tropical specimen which is said ( ) have been living in captivity for 25 years.
6. They find convenient places in which to dig their burrows and spend the rest of their lives ( ) solitude.
7. The entire body of a tarantula, especially its legs, is thickly clothed ( ) hair.
8. ( ) the touch of a cricket's antennae the tarantula seizes the insect very swiftly.
9. These three tactile responses are so different from one another ( ) there is no possibility of confusing them.
10. The sting is much worse than ( ) of a bee or common wasp, and the pain and swelling last longer.
11. The female produces but a few eggs, one at a time ( ) intervals of two or three days.
12. The sex of the spider ( ) no difference, but the mother is highly discriminating as to species.
13. Now and again, the wasp pops out of the hole to ( ) sure that the spider is still there.
14. Now at last the harassed spider tries a desperate ( ) vain defense.
15. She stays there for several hours, and ( ) she does all that

time in the dark we do not know.

16. This is not to say that instinct ( ) no part or that she reasons as man does.
17. We do not know ( ) certain how she identifies the tarantula but she does it purposefully and does not blindly tackle a wrong species.

D. *Choose one of the words that best fits each of the following sentences.*

a. initiative	b. inflicted	c. stimulating	d. disturb
e. mammals	f. exasperated	g. stimulating	h. cylindrical

1. The judge ( ) the severest possible penalty.
2. Humans and dogs are ( ); birds and fish are not.
3. Beer cans are ( ).
4. I asked him a question but he gave no ( ).
5. I find swimming the most ( ) form of exercise.
6. I'm sorry to ( ) you, but could you tell me how this machine works?
7. I was ( ) by all the delays.
8. He took the ( ) in organizing a party after his brother's wedding.

16. The Value of Philosophy

BERTRAND RUSSELL*

It will be well to consider what is the value of philosophy and why it ought to be studied. It is the more necessary to consider this question, in view of the fact that many men, under the influence of science or of practical affairs, are inclined to doubt whether philosophy is anything better than innocent but useless trifling, hair-splitting[1] distinctions, and controversies on matters concerning which knowledge is impossible.

This view of philosophy appears to result, partly from a wrong conception of the ends of life, partly from a wrong conception of the kind of goods which philosophy strives to achieve. Physical science, through the medium of inventions, is useful to innumerable people who are wholly ignorant of it; thus the study of physical science is to be recommended, not only, or primarily, because of the effect on the student, but rather because of the effect on mankind in general. This utility does not belong to philosophy. If the study of philosophy has any value at all for others than students of philosophy, it must be only indirectly,

---

* **Bertrand Russell(1872~1970):** 영국의 수학자, 철학가, 문화 비평가. 1950년에 Nobel문학상을 수상. 대표작으로는 History of Western Philosophy, The Principles of Mathematics등이 있음.

1. concerned with subtle but petty distinctions

through its effects upon the lives of those who study it. It is in these effects, therefore, if anywhere, that the value of philosophy must be primarily sought.

But further, if we are not to fail in our endeavor to determine the value of philosophy, we must first free our minds from the prejudices of what are wrongly called "practical" men. The "practical" man, as this word is often used, is one who recognizes only material needs, who realizes that men must have food for the body, but is oblivious of the necessity of providing food for the mind. If all men were well off, if poverty and disease had been reduced to their lowest possible point, there would still remain much to be done to produce a valuable society; and even in the existing world the goods of the mind are at least as important as the goods of the body. It is exclusively among the goods of the mind that the value of philosophy is to be found; and only those who are not indifferent to these goods can be persuaded that the study of philosophy is not a waste of time.

Philosophy, like all other studies, aims primarily at knowledge. The knowledge it aims at is the kind of knowledge which gives unity and system to the body of the sciences, and the kind which results from a critical examination of the grounds of our convictions, prejudices, and beliefs. But it cannot be maintained that philosophy has had any very great measure of success in its attempts to provide definite answers to its questions. If you ask a mathematician, a mineralogist, a historian, or any other man of learning, what definite body of truths has been ascertained by his science, his answer will last as long as you are willing to listen. But if you put the same question to a philosopher, he will, if he is candid, have to confess that his study has not achieved positive results such as have been achieved by other sciences. It is true that this is partly accounted for by the fact that, as soon as definite knowledge concerning any subject becomes possible, this subject ceases to be called philosophy, and becomes a separate science. The whole study of the heavens, which now belongs to astronomy, was once included in philosophy; Newton's great work was called "the mathematical principles of natural philosophy." Similarly, the study of the human mind, which was a part of philosophy, has now been separated from philosophy and has become the science of psychology. Thus, to a great extent, the uncertainty of philosophy is more apparent than real: those questions which are already capable of definite answers are placed in the sciences, while those only to which, at present, no definite answer can be given, remain to form the residue which is called philosophy.

This is, however, only a part of the truth concerning the uncertainty of philosophy. There are many questions—and among them those that are of the profoundest interest to our spiritual life—which, so far as we can see, must remain insoluble to the human intellect unless its powers become of quite a different order from what they are now. Has the universe any unity of plan or purpose, or is it a fortuitous concourse of atoms? Is consciousness a permanent part of the universe, giving hope of indefinite growth in wisdom, or is it a transitory accident on a small planet on which life must ultimately become impossible? Are good and evil of importance to the universe or only to man? Such questions are asked by philosophy, and variously answered by various philosophers. But it would seem that, whether answers be otherwise discoverable or not, the answers suggested by philosophy are none of them demonstrably[2] true. Yet, however

2. capable of being shown or proved

slight may be the hope of discovering an answer, it is part of the business of philosophy to continue the consideration of such questions, to make us aware of their importance, to examine all the approaches to them, and to keep alive that speculative interest in the universe which is apt to be killed by confining ourselves to definitely ascertainable knowledge.

Many philosophers, it is true, have held that philosophy could establish the truth of certain answers to such fundamental questions. They have supposed that what is of most importance in religious beliefs could be proved by strict demonstration to be true. In order to judge of such attempts, it is necessary to take a survey of human knowledge, and to form an opinion as to its methods and its limitations. On such a subject it would be unwise to pronounce dogmatically; but if our investigations do not lead us astray, we shall be compelled to renounce the hope of finding philosophical proofs of religious beliefs. We cannot, therefore, include as part of the value of philosophy any definite set of answers to such questions. Hence, once more, the value of philosophy must not depend upon any supposed body of definitely ascertainable knowledge to be acquired by those who study it.

The value of philosophy is, in fact, to be sought largely in its very uncertainty. The man who has no tincture of philosophy goes through life imprisoned in the prejudices derived from common sense, from the habitual beliefs of his age or his nation, and from convictions which have grown up in his mind without the co-operation or consent of his deliberate reason. To such a man the world tends to become definite, finite, obvious; common objects rouse no questions, and unfamiliar possibilities are contemptuously rejected. As soon as we begin to philosophize, on the contrary, we find that even the most everyday things lead to problems to which only very incomplete answers can be given. Philosophy, though unable to tell us with certainty what is the true answer to the doubts which it raises, is able to suggest many possibilities which enlarge our thoughts and free them from the tyranny of custom. Thus, while diminishing our feeling of certainty as to what things are, it greatly increases our knowledge as to what they may be; it removes the somewhat arrogant dogmatism of those who have never traveled into the region of liberating doubt, and it keeps alive our sense of wonder by showing familiar things in an unfamiliar aspect.

Apart from its utility in showing unsuspected possibilities, philosophy has a value—perhaps its chief value—through the greatness of the objects which it contemplates, and the freedom from narrow and personal aims resulting from this contemplation. The life of the instinctive man is shut up within the circle of his private interests: family and friends may be included, but the outer world is not regarded except as it may help or hinder what comes within the circle of his instinctive wishes. In such a life there is something feverish and confined, in comparison with the philosophic life which is calm and free. The private world of instinctive interests is a small one, set in the midst of a great and powerful world which must, sooner or later, lay our private world in ruins. Unless we can so enlarge our interests as to include the whole outer world, we remain like a garrison in a beleaguered fortress, knowing that the enemy prevents escape and that ultimate surrender is inevitable. In such a life there is no peace, but a constant strife between the insistence of desire and powerlessness of will. In one way or another, if our life is to be great and free, we must escape this prison and this strife.

One way of escape is by philosophic contemplation. Philosophic contemplation does not, in its widest survey, divide the universe into two hostile camps—friends and foes, helpful and hostile, good and bad—it views the whole impartially. Philosophic contemplation, when it is unalloyed, does not aim at proving that the rest of the universe is akin to man. All acquisition of knowledge is an enlargement of the Self, but this enlargement is best attained when it is not directly sought. It is obtained when the desire for knowledge is alone operative, by a study which does not wish in advance that its objects should have this or that character, but adapts the Self to the characters which it finds in its objects. This enlargement of Self is not obtained when, taking the Self as it is, we try to show that the world is so similar to this Self that knowledge of it is possible without any admission of what seems alien. The desire to prove this is a form of self-assertion, and like all self-assertion, it is an obstacle to the growth of Self which it desires, and of which the Self knows that it is capable. Self-assertion, in philosophic speculation as elsewhere, views the world as a means to its own ends; thus it makes the world of less account[3] than Self, and the Self sets bounds to[4] the greatness of its goods. In contemplation, on the contrary, we start from the not-Self, and through its greatness the boundaries of Self are enlarged; through the infinity of the universe the mind which contemplates it achieves some share in infinity.

For this reason greatness of soul is not fostered by those philosophies which assimilate the universe to Man. Knowledge is a form of union of Self and not-Self, like all union, it is impaired by dominion, and therefore by any attempt to force the universe into conformity with what we find in ourselves. There is a

3. less important
4. limit

widespread philosophical tendency towards the view which tells us that Man is the measure of all things, that truth is man-made, that space and time and the world of universals are properties of the mind, and that, if there be anything not created by the mind, it is unknowable and of no account for us. This view, if our previous discussions were correct, is untrue; but in addition to being untrue, it has the effect of robbing philosophic contemplation of all that gives it value, since it fetters contemplation to Self. What it calls knowledge is not a union with the not-Self, but a set of prejudices, habits, and desires, making an impenetrable veil between us and the world beyond. The man who finds pleasure in such a theory of knowledge is like the man who never leaves the domestic circle for fear his word might not be law.

The true philosophic contemplation, on the contrary, finds its satisfaction in every enlargement of the not-Self, in everything that magnifies the objects contemplated, and thereby the subject contemplating. Everything, in contemplation, that is personal or private, everything that depends upon habit, self-interest, or desire, distorts the object, and hence impairs the union which the intellect seeks. By thus making a barrier between subject and object, such personal and private things become a prison to the intellect. The free intellect will see as God might see, without a *here* and *now*[5], without hopes and fears, without the trammels of customary beliefs and traditional prejudices, calmly, dispassionately, in the sole and exclusive desire of knowledge—knowledge as impersonal, as purely contemplative, as it is possible for man to attain. Hence also the free intellect will value more the abstract and universal knowledge into which the accidents of private

5. 현실세계의 시간과 공간을 초월하여

history do not enter, than the knowledge brought by the senses, and dependent, as such knowledge must be, upon an exclusive and personal point of view and a body whose sense-organs distort as much as they reveal.

The mind which has become accustomed to the freedom and impartiality of philosophic contemplation will preserve something of the same freedom and impartiality in the world of action and emotion. It will view its purposes and desires as parts of the whole, with the absence of insistence that results from seeing them as infinitesimal fragments in a world of which all the rest is unaffected by any one man's deeds. The impartiality which, in contemplation, is the unalloyed desire for truth, is the very same quality of mind which, in action, is justice, and in emotion is that universal love which can be given to all, and not only to those who are judged useful or admirable. Thus contemplation enlarges not only the objects of our thoughts, but also the object of our actions and our affections: it makes us citizens of the universe, not only of one walled city at war with all the rest. In this citizenship of the universe consists man's true freedom, and his liberation from the thralldom of narrow hopes and fears.

Thus, to sum up our discussion of the value of philosophy: philosophy is to be studied, not for the sake of any definite answers to its questions, since no definite answers can, as a rule, be known to be true, but rather for the sake of the questions themselves; because these questions enlarge our conception of what is possible, enrich our intellectual imagination, and diminish the dogmatic assurance which closes the mind against speculation; but above all because, through the greatness of the universe which philosophy contemplates, the mind is rendered great, and becomes capable of that union with the universe which constitutes its highest good.

EXERCISES

A. *Answer the following questions.*

1. How does the author develop the distinction between instinctive and philosophical thought?
2. What is the true philosophy that sets us free?
3. Can philosophy supply true answers to fundamental questions?
4. Why should we ask about the value of philosophy?
5. What is the final answer to our question about the value of philosophy?

B. *Match the words in the left-hand column to the most suitable meaning from the right-hand column.*

1. assertion	control
2. assimilate	of little value
3. dominion	to make a great effort
4. fortuitous	a forceful statement
5. transitory	not caring about
6. diminishing	truthful
7. indifferent	what is left
8. hair-splitting	that cannot be explained
9. trifling	accidental
10. deliberate	lasting only a short time
11. residue	intentional
12. instinctive	making smaller

13. contemplate	to think about
14. strive	natural, without prior thought
15. candid	to redefine something to make it fit a system
16. insoluble	paying too much attention to small unnecessary differences

C. *Choose one of the words that best fits each of the following sentences.*

a. conception	b. impartiality	c. practical
d. contemplation	e. measure	f. profoundest
g. consciousness	h. indefinite	i. compelled
j. dogmatism	k. unsuspected	l. feverish
m. infinitesimal	n.influence	

1. The monks spent an hour in _______ each morning.
2. He promised to use his _______ with the chairman to get me the job.
3. He has not become rich but he has had a _______ of success.
4. The old man lost _______ at eight o'clock and died a few hours later.
5. I shall be _______ to leave if that woman comes in here.
6. He has got a strange _______ of friendship. He just bit her.
7. I offered my _______ apologies when I saw what had happened.
8. They have agreed to store the furniture; but we still have the _______ problem of how to transport it over there.
9. Even an _______ amount of this chemical in the water will poison the entire population of a city.

10. The judge showed his _______ by awarding the prize to the unpopular competitor.
11. There is an _______ ban on the sale of ivory. It is most unlikely to be lifted.
12. They won't accept your advice. They have a terrible _______ about bringing up their children.
13. His criminal tendencies went _______ right up to the day when they caught him stealing.
14. Time was running out. They worked with _______ haste to finish the job.

CHILDREN LEARN WHAT THEY LIVE

If a child lives with criticism, he learns to condemn.
If a child lives with hostility, he learns to fight.
If a child lives with ridicule, he learns to be shy.
If a child lives with shame, he learns to feel guilty.
If a child lives with tolerance, he learns to be patient.
If a child lives with encouragement, he learns confidence.
If a child lives with praise, he learns to appreciate.
If a child lives with fairness, he learns justice.
If a child lives with security, he learns to have faith.
If a child lives with approval, he learns to like himself.
If a child lives with acceptance and friendship,
He learns to find love in the world.

Dorothy Law Nolte

17. New York

GAY TALESE*

New York is a city of things unnoticed. It is a city with cats sleeping under parked cars, two stone armadillos crawling up St. Patrick's Cathedral, and thousands of ants creeping on top of the Empire State Building. The ants probably were carried up there by wind or birds, but nobody is sure; nobody in New York knows any more about the ants than they do about the panhandler who takes taxis to the Bowery[1]; or the dapper man who picks trash out of Sixth Avenue trash cans; or the medium in the West Seventies who claims, "I am clairvoyant, clairaudient, and clairsensuous."

New York is a city for eccentrics and a center for odd bits of information. New Yorkers blink twenty-eight times a minute, but forty when tense. Most popcorn chewers at Yankee Stadium stop chewing momentarily just before the pitch. Gumchewers on Macy's[2] escalators stop chewing momentarily just before they get off — to concentrate on the last step. Coins, paper clips, ball-point pens, and little girls' pocketbooks are found by workmen when they clean the sea lion's pool at the Bronx Zoo.

---

* **Gay Talese: (1932～):** 미국의 언론인, New York Times 기자 역임(1955～1965), The Kingdom and the Power(1969)등의 저서가 있음.

1. New York의 East Side 의 한 거리
2. 미국의 큰 백화점

A Park Avenue doorman has parts of three bullets in his head —there since World War I. Several young gypsy daughters, influenced by television and literacy, are running away from home because they don't want to grow up and become fortune-tellers. Each month a hundred pounds of hair is delivered to Louis Feder on 545 Fifth Avenue, where blond hairpieces are made from German women's hair; brunette hairpieces from Italian women's hair; but no hairpieces from American women's hair which, says Mr. Feder, is weak from too frequent rinses and permanents.

Some of New York's best informed men are elevator operators, who rarely talk, but always listen—like doormen. Sardi's doormen listen to the comments made by Broadway's first-nighters walking by after the last act. They listen closely. They listen carefully. Within ten minutes they can tell you which shows will flop[3] and which will be hits.

On Broadway each evening a big, dark, 1948 Rolls-Royce[4] pulls into Forty-sixth Street—and out hop two little ladies armed with Bibles and signs reading, "The Dammed Shall Perish." These ladies proceed to stand on the corner screaming at the multitudes of Broadway sinners, sometimes until three a.m., when their chauffeur in the Rolls picks them up and drives them back to Westchester.

By this time Fifth Avenue is deserted by all but a few strolling insomniacs, some cruising cabdrivers, and a group of sophisticated females who stand in store windows all night and day wearing cold, perfect smiles. Like sentries they line Fifth Avenue—these window mannequins who gaze onto the quiet street with tilted heads and pointed toes and long rubber fingers reaching for

3. (공연 등이) fail, unsuccessful
4. 영국 Rolls-Royce사가 제조한 고급 승용차

cigarettes that aren't there.

At five a.m. Manhattan is a town of tired trumpet players and homeward-bound bartenders. Pigeons control Park Avenue and strut unchallenged in the middle of the street. This is Manhattan's mellowest hour. Most *night* people are out of sight—but the *day* people have not yet appeared. Truck drivers and cabs are alert, yet they do not disturb the mood. They do not disturb the abandoned Rockefeller Center, or the motionless night watchmen in the Fulton Fish Market, or the gas-station attendant sleeping next to Sloppy Louie's with the radio on.

At five a.m. the Broadway regulars either have gone home or to all-night coffee shops where, under the glaring light, you see their whiskers and wear. And on Fifty-first Street a radio press car is parked at the curb with a photographer who has nothing to do. So he just sits there for a few nights, looks through the windshield, and soon becomes a keen observer of life after midnight.

"At one a.m.," he says, "Broadway is filled with wise guys and with kids coming out of the Astor Hotel in white dinner jackets—kids who drive to dances in their fathers' cars. You also see cleaning ladies going home, always wearing kerchiefs. By two a.m. some of the drinkers are getting out of hand[5], and this is the hour for bar fights. At three a.m. the last show is over in the nightclubs, and most of the tourists and out-of-town buyers are back in hotels. And small-time comedians are criticizing big-time comedians in Hanson's Drugstore. At four a.m., after the bars close, you see the drunks come out—and also the pimps and prostitutes who take advantage of drunks. At five a.m., though, it is mostly quiet. New York is an entirely different city at five a.m."

---

5. 걷잡을 수 없게 되다

At six a.m. the early workers begin to push up from the subways. The traffic begins to move down Broadway like a river. And Mrs. Mary Woody jumps out of bed, dashes to her office, and phones dozens of sleepy New Yorkers to say in a cheerful voice, rarely appreciated: "Good morning. Time to get up." For twenty years, as an operator of Western Union's Wake-Up Service, Mrs. Woody has gotten millions out of bed.

By seven a.m. a floridly robust little man, looking very Parisian in a blue beret and turtleneck sweater, moves in a hurried step along Park Avenue visiting his wealthy lady friends—making certain that each is given a brisk, before-breakfast rubdown. The uniformed doormen greet him warmly and call him either "Biz" or "Mac" because he is Biz Mackey, a ladies' masseur *extraordinaire*. He never reveals the names of his customers, but most of them are middle-aged and rich. He visits each of them in their apartments, and has special keys to their bedrooms; he is often the first man they see in the morning, and they lie in bed waiting for him.

The doormen that Biz passes each morning are generally an obliging, endlessly articulate group of sidewalk diplomats who list among their friends some of Manhattan's most powerful men, most beautiful women, and snootiest poodles. More often than not, the doormen are big, slightly Gothic in design, and the possessors of eyes sharp enough to spot big tippers a block away in the year's thickest fog. Some East Side doormen are as proud as grandees, and their uniforms, heavily festooned, seem to come from the same tailor who outfitted Marshal Tito[6].

Shortly after seven-thirty each morning hundreds of people are lined along Forty-second Street waiting for the eight a.m. opening

---

6. Marshal Tito(1892～1980): Yugoslavia의 총리 및 대통령(1953～1980)

of the ten movie houses that stand almost shoulder-to-shoulder between Times Square and Eighth Avenue. Who are these people who go to the movies at eight a.m.? They are the city's insomniacs, night watchmen, and people who can't go home, do not want to go home, or have no home. They are derelicts, homosexuals, cops, hacks, truck drivers, cleaning ladies, and restaurant men who have worked all night. They are also alcoholics who are waiting for eight a.m. to pay their forty cents for a soft seat and to sleep in the dark, smoky theater. And yet, aside from being smoky, each of Times Square's theaters has a special quality, or lack of quality, about it. At the Victory Theater one finds horror films, while at the Times Square Theater they feature only cowboy films. There are first-run films[7] for forty cents at the Lyric, while at the Selwyn there are always second-run films for thirty cents. But if you go to the Apollo Theater you will see, in addition to foreign films, people in the lobby talking with their hands. These are deaf-and-dumb movie fans who patronize the Apollo because they read the subtitles. The Apollo probably has the biggest deaf-and-dumb movie audience in the world.

New York is a city of 38,000 cabdrivers, 10,000 bus drivers, but only one chauffeur who has a chauffeur. The wealthy chauffeur can be seen driving up Fifth Avenue each morning, and his name is Roosevelt Zanders. He earns $100,000 a year, is a gentleman of impeccable taste and, although he owns a $23,000 Rolls-Royce, does not scorn his friends who own Bentleys[8]. For $150 a day, Mr. Zanders will drive anyone anywhere in his big, silver Rolls. Diplomats patronize him, models pose next to him,

---

7. 개봉 영화
8. a very expensive British car

and each day he receives cables from around the world urging that he be waiting at Idlewild, on the docks, or outside the Plaza Hotel. Sometimes at night, however, he is too tired to drive anymore. So Bob Clarke, his chauffeur, takes over and Mr. Zanders relaxes in the back.

New York is a town of 3,000 bootblacks whose brushes and rhythmic ragsnaps can be heard up and down Manhattan from midmorning to midnight. They dodge cops, survive rainstorms, and thrive in the Empire State Building as well as on the Staten Island Ferry. They usually wear dirty shoes.

New York is a city of headless men who sit obscurely in subway booths all day and night selling tokens to people in a hurry. Each weekday more than 4,500,000 riders pass these money changers who seem to have neither heads, faces, nor personalities — only fingers. Except when giving directions, their vocabulary consists largely of three words: "How many, please?"

In New York there are 200 chestnut vendors, and they average $25 on a good day peddling soft, warm chestnuts. Like many vendors, the chestnut men do not own their own rigs—they borrow or rent them from pushcart makers such as David Amerman.

Mr. Amerman, with offices opposite a defunct public bathhouse on the Lower East Side, is New York's master builder of pushcarts. His father and grandfather before him were pushcart makers, and the family has long been a household word among the city's most discriminating junkmen, fruit vendors, and hot-dog peddlers.

In New York there are 500 mediums, ranging from semi-trance to trance to deep-trance types. Most of them live in New York's West Seventies and Eighties, and on Sundays some of these blocks are communicating with the dead, vibrating to trumpets, and solving all problems.

The Manhattan Telephone Directory has 776,300 names, of which 3,316 are Smith, 2,835 are Brown, 2,444 are Williams, 2,070 are Cohen—and one is Mike Krasilovsky. Any one who doubts this last fact has only to look at the top of page 876 where, in large black letters, is this sign: "There is only one Mike Krasilovsky. Sterling 3-1990."

In New York the Fifth Avenue Lingerie shop is on Madison Avenue; the Madison Pet Shop is on Lexington Avenue; the Park Avenue Florist is on Madison Avenue; and the Lexington Hand Laundry is on Third Avenue. New York is the home of 120 pawnbrokers and it is where Bishop Sheen's brother, Dr. Sheen, shares an office with one Dr. Bishop.

New York is a town of thirty tattooists where interest in mankind is skin-deep, but whose impressions usually last a lifetime. Each day the tattooists go pecking away over acres of anatomy. And in downtown Manhattan, Stanley Moskowitz, a scion of a distinguished family of Bowery skin-peckers, does a grand business.

When it rains in Manhattan, automobile traffic is slow, dates are broken and, in hotel lobbies, people slump behind newspapers or walk aimlessly about with no place to sit, nobody to talk to, nothing to do. Taxis are harder to get; department stores do between fifteen and twenty-five percent less business, and the monkeys in the Bronx Zoo, having no audience, slouch grumpily in their cages looking more bored than the lobby-loungers.

While some New Yorkers become morose with rain, others prefer it, like to walk in it, and say that on rainy days the city's buildings seem somehow cleaner—washed in an opalescence, like a Monet painting. There are fewer suicides in New York when it rains. But when the sun is shining, and New Yorkers seem happy, the depressed person sinks deeper into depression, and Bellevue

Hospital gets more suicide calls.

New York is a town of 8,485 telephone operators, 1,364 Western Union messenger boys, and 112 newspaper copy-boys. An average baseball crowd at Yankee Stadium uses over ten gallons of liquid soap per game—an unofficial high mark for cleanliness in the major leagues; the stadium also has the league's top number of ushers (360), sweepers (72), and men's rooms (34).

New York is a town in which the brotherhood of Russian Bath Rubbers, the only union advocating sweatshops, appears to be heading for its last rubdown. The union has been going in New York City for years, but now most of the rubbers are pushing seventy[9] and are deaf—from all the water and the hot temperatures.

Each afternoon in New York a rather seedy saxophone player, his cheeks blown out like a spinnaker, stands on the sidewalk playing *Danny Boy* in such a sad, sensitive way that he soon has half the neighborhood peeking out of windows tossing nickels, dimes, and quarters at his feet. Some of the coins roll under parked cars, but most of them are caught in his outstretched hand. The saxophone player is a street musician named Joe Gabler; for the past thirty years he has serenaded every block in New York and has sometimes been tossed as much as $100 a day in coins. He is also hit with buckets of water, empty beer cans and eggs, and chased by wild dogs. He is believed to be the last of New York's ancient street musicians.

New York is a town of nineteen midget wrestlers. They all can squeeze into the Hotel Holland's elevator, six can sleep in one bed, eight can be comfortably transported to Madison Square Garden in the chauffeur-driven Cadillac reserved for the midget wrestlers.

---

9. 70세가 가까워 오다

In New York from dawn to dusk to dawn, day after day, you can hear the steady rumble of tires against the concrete span of George Washington Bridge. The bridge is never completely still. It trembles with traffic. It moves in the wind. Its great veins of steel swell when hot and contract when cold; its span often is ten feet closer to the Hudson River in summer than in winter. It is an almost restless structure of graceful beauty which, like an irresistible seductress, withholds secrets from the romantics who gaze upon it, the escapists who jump off it, the chubby girl who lumbers across its 3,500-foot span trying to reduce, and the 100,000 motorists who each day cross it, smash into it, shortchange it, get jammed up on it.

When street traffic dwindles and most people are sleeping in New York, some neighborhoods begin to crawl with cats. They move quickly through the shadows of buildings; night watchmen, policemen, garbage collectors, and other nocturnal wanderers see them—but never for long.

There are 200, 000 stray cats in New York. A majority of them hang around the fish market, or in Greenwich Village, and in the East and West Side neighborhoods where garbage cans abound. No part of the city is without its strays, however, and all-night garage attendants in such busy neighborhoods as Fifty-fourth Street have counted as many as twenty of them around the Ziegfeld Theater early in the morning. Troops of cats patrol the waterfront piers at night searching for rats. Subway trackwalkers have discovered cats living in the darkness. They seem never to get hit by trains, though some are occasionally liquidated by the third rail[10]. About twenty-five cats live seventy-five feet below the

10. 전차의 제3궤조(송전용)

west end of Grand Central Terminal, are fed by the underground workers, and never wander up into the daylight.

New York is a city in which large, cliff-dwelling hawks cling to skyscrapers and occasionally zoom to snatch a pigeon over Central Park, or Wall Street, or the Hudson River. Bird watchers have seen these peregrine falcons circling lazily over the city. They have seen them perched atop tall buildings, even around Times Square. About twelve of these hawks patrol the city, sometimes with a wingspan of thirty-five inches. They have buzzed women on the roof of the St. Regis Hotel, have attacked repairmen on smokestacks, and, in August, 1947, two hawks jumped women residents in the recreation yard of the Home of the New York Guild for the Jewish Blind. Maintenance men at the Riverside Church have seen hawks dining on pigeons in the bell tower. The hawks remain there for only a little while. And then they fly out to the river, leaving pigeons' heads for the Riverside maintenance men to clean up. When the hawks return, they fly in quietly — *unnoticed*, like the cats, the headless men, the ants, the ladies' masseur, the doorman with three bullets in his head, and most of the other offbeat wonders in this town without time.

EXERCISES

A. *Answer the following questions.*

1. What does the first sentence imply?
2. Does the author describe the typical tourist attractions of New York? Why?
3. Is the image of New York presented in this essay basically

positive or negative?
4. What are your impressions of New York from this essay?
5. Do you think the author likes New York? Why?

B. *Give the correct forms of the words given in the brackets.*
1. Most popcorn chewers at Yankee Stadium stop chewing (momentary) just before the pitch.
2. Pigeons control Park Avenue and strut (challenge) in the middle of the street.
3. The doormen that Biz passes each morning are generally an (oblige), endlessly articulate group of sidewalk diplomats.
4. Except when (give) directions, their vocabulary consists largely of three words: "How many, please?"
5. Each day the tattooists go (peck) away over acres of anatomy.
6. The monkeys in the Bronx Zoo, having no audience, slouch grumpily in their cages (look) more bored than the lobby-loungers.
7. The brotherhood of Russian Bath Rubbers, the only union (advocate) sweatshops, appears to be heading for its last rubdown.
8. Some of the coins roll under parked cars, but most of them (catch) in his outstretched hand.
9. It is an almost restless structure of graceful beauty which, like an (resist) seductress, withholds secrets from the romantics who gaze upon it.
10. Bird watchers have seen these peregrine falcons circling (lazy) over the city.
11. They have seen them (perch) atop tall buildings, even around Times Square.

C. *Fill in the blanks with suitable words.*
1. New York is a city (   ) cats sleeping under parked cars,

two stone armadillos crawling up St. Patrick's Cathedral.

2. Sardi's doormen listen to the comments ( ) by Broadway's first-nighters walking by after the last act.
3. Their chauffeur in the Rolls-Royce picks them ( ) and drives them back to Westchester.
4. By this time Fifth Avenue is deserted by all ( ) a few strolling insomniacs.
5. By two a.m. some of the drinkers are getting ( ) of hand, and this is the hour for bar fights.
6. A floridly robust little man, looking very Parisian ( ) a blue beret and turtleneck sweater, moves in a hurried step along Park Avenue.
7. They dodge cops, survive rainstorms, and thrive ( ) the Empire State Building as well as on the Staten Island Ferry.
8. New York is a town of nineteen midget wrestlers. They all can squeeze ( ) the Hotel Holland's elevator.
9. When street traffic dwindles and most people are sleeping in New York, some neighborhoods begin to crawl ( ) cats.
10. A majority of the stray cats in New York hang ( ) the fish market or in Greenwich Village.

D. *Choose one of the words that best fits each of the following sentences.*

a. appreciated	b. eccentric	c. chauffeuring
d. patronize	e. literacy	f. panhandled

1. A slouching bum near his office ( ) him that afternoon.
2. If you go to the palace in sandals, they will think you are rather ( ).
3. A country cannot be considered really modernized unless its

(   ) rate is fairy close to 100 percent.
4. You father should not waste his time (   ) your around; you will have to learn to drive yourself.
5. Her remarkable ability to get things done was not (   ) in her job.
6. I will not (   ) this store any more; the assistants are so rude.

YOUTH

Youth is not a time of life; it is a state of mind; it is not a matter of rosy cheeks, red lips and supple knees; it is a matter of the will, a quality of the imagination, a vigor of the emotions; it is the freshness of the deep springs of life.

Youth means a temperamental predominance of courage over timidity, of the appetite for adventure over the love of ease. This often exists in a man of 60 more than a boy of 20. Nobody grows old merely by a number of years. We grow old by deserting our ideals.

Years may wrinkle the skin, but to give up enthusiasm wrinkles the soul. Worry, fear, self-distrust bows the heart and turns the spirit back to dust.

Whether 60 or 16, there is in every human being's heart the lure of wonder, the unfailing child-like appetite of what's next and the joy of the game of living. In the center of our heart and my heart there is a wireless station: so long as it receives messages of beauty, hope, cheer, courage and power from men and from the Infinite, so long are you young.

When the aerials are down, and your spirit is covered with snows of cynicism and the ice of pessimism, then you are grown old, even at 20, but as long as your aerials are up, to catch waves of optimism, there is hope you may die young at 80.

Samuel Ullman

18. Symptoms

JEROME K. JEROME*

It was my liver that was out of order. I knew it was my liver that was out of order, because I had just been reading a patent liver-pill circular, in which were detailed the various symptoms by which a man could tell when his liver was out of order. I had them all.

It is a most extraordinary thing, but I never read a patent medicine advertisement without being impelled to the conclusion that I am suffering from the particular disease therein dealt with in its most virulent form. The diagnosis seems in every case to correspond exactly with all the sensations that I have ever felt.

I remember going to the British Museum[1] one day to read up the treatment for some slight ailment of which I had a touch—hay fever, I fancy it was. I got down the book, and read all I came to read; and then, in an unthinking moment[2], I idly turned the leaves, and began to indolently study diseases, generally. I forget which was the first distemper I plunged into—some fearful, devastating scourge, I know—and, before I had glanced half down the list of 'premonitory

---

* **Jerome K. Jerome(1859～1927):** 영국의 수필가, 소설가, 극작가. 작품으로 'Three Men in a Boat' 가 있음

1. British museum 에는 큰 도서관이 있음
2. when I was not paying much attention to what I was doing

symptoms', it was borne in upon me that I had fairly got it[3].

I sat for a while, frozen with horror; and then, in the listlessness of despair, I again turned over the pages. I came to typhoid fever—read the symptoms—discovered that I had typhoid fever, must have had it for months without knowing it—wondered what else I had got; turned up St Vitus's Dance[4]—found, as I expected, that I had that too—began to get interested in my case, and determined to sift it to the bottom, and so started alphabetically—read up ague, and learned that I was sickening for it, and that the acute stage would commence in about another fortnight. Bright's disease[5], I was relieved to find, I had only in a modified form, and, so far as that was concerned, I might live for years. Cholera I had, with severe complications; and diphtheria I seemed to have been born with. I plodded conscientiously through the twenty-six letters, and the only malady I could conclude I had not got was housemaid's knee[6].

I felt rather hurt about this at first, it seemed somehow to be a sort of slight. Why hadn't I got housemaid's knee? Why this invidious reservation? After a while, however, less grasping feelings prevailed[7]. I reflected that I had every other known malady in the pharmacology, and I grew less selfish, and determined to do without housemaid's knee. Gout in its most malignant stage, it would appear, had seized me without my being aware of it; and zymosis I had evidently been suffering with from boyhood. There were no more diseases after zymosis, so I

---

3. I realized that I was certainly suffering from that disease
4. 무도병(근육경련을 일으키는 신경병의 일종)
5. 신장염
6. 슬개골 활액낭염(무릎을 꿇는 일이 많아 생기는 병)
7. I no longer felt I ought to have every disease in the book

concluded there was nothing else the matter with me.

I sat and pondered. I thought what an interesting case I must be from a medical point of view, what an acquisition I should be to a class! Students would have no need to 'walk the hospitals', if they had me. I was a hospital in myself. All they need do would be to walk round me, and, after that, take their diploma.

Then I wondered how long I had to live. I tried to examine myself. I felt my pulse. I could not at first find any pulse at all. Then, all of a sudden, it seemed to start off. I pulled out my watch and timed it. I made it a hundred and forty-seven to the minute. I tried to feel my heart. I could not feel my heart. It had stopped beating. I have since been induced to come to the opinion that it must have been there all the time, and must have been beating, but I can not account for it. I patted myself all over my front, from what I call my waist up to my head, and I went a bit round each side, and a little way up the back. But I could not feel or hear anything. I tried to look at my tongue. I stuck it out as far as ever it would go, and I shut one eye, and tried to examine it with the other. I could only see the tip, and the only thing that I could gain from that was to feel more certain than before that I had scarlet fever.

I had walked into that reading-room a happy, healthy man. I crawled out a decrepit wreck.

I went to my medical man. He is an old chum of mine, and feels my pulse, and looks at my tongue, and talks about the weather, all for nothing, when I fancy I'm ill; so I thought I would do him a good turns[8] by going to him now. 'What a doctor wants,' I said, 'is practice. He shall have me. He will get more practice out of me than out of seventeen hundred of your ordinary commonplace patients,

---

8. do something to help him

with only one or two diseases each.' So I went straight up and saw him, and he said: 'Well, what's the matter with you?'

I said: 'I will not take up your time, dear boy, with telling you what is the matter with me. Life is brief, and you might pass away before I had finished. But I will tell you what is not the matter with me. I have not got housemaid's knee. Why I have not got housemaid's knee, I can not tell you; but the fact remains that I have not got it. Everything else, however, I have got.'

And I told him how I came to discover it all.

Then he opened me and looked down me, and clutched hold of my wrist, and then he hit me over the chest when I wasn't expecting it—a cowardly thing to do, I call it—and immediately afterwards butted me with the side of his head. After that, he sat down and wrote out a prescription, and folded it up and gave it to me, and I put it in my pocket and went out.

I did not open it. I took it to the nearest chemist's and handed it in. The man read it, and then handed it back.

He said he didn't keep it.

I said: 'You are a chemist?'

He said: 'I am a chemist. If I was a cooperative store and family hotel combined, I might be able to oblige you. Being only a chemist hampers me.'

I read the prescription. It ran:

1 1b beefsteak, with

1 pt bitter beer every 6 hours.

1 ten-mile walk every morning.

1 bed at 11 sharp every night.

And don't stuff your head with things you don't understand.

I followed the directions, with the happy result—speaking for myself—that my life was preserved, and is still going on.

EXERCISES

A. *Answer the following questions.*

1. Is the character in the story really ill?
2. Does the author make fun of himself? Why?
3. Do you think the essay is humourous?
4. What does the author try to tell about people's habit of worrying about imagined illnesses?

B. *Read the following statements based on the essay. Write "T" if a statement is true, and "F" if it is false.*

1. The doctor was an old man to whom the author often went.
2. The doctor did not usually accept any fee from the author.
3. The author admits that he sometimes imagined that he had something wrong with him.
4. ' ...and talks about the weather...' This shows that the doctor did not take the author's complaint seriously.
5. The author thought he was obliging the doctor by going to see him on this occasion.
6. The author says 'Life is brief'. He means that he may not live long enough to describe all the diseases he has.
7. The author talks as if he has failed in some way by not having housemaid's knee.
8. 'I told him how I came to discover it all.' This shows that the author had come to the doctor to find out what diseases he had.
9. The doctor probably unbuttoned the author's shirt.
10. The doctor was a cowardly man.
11. The doctor was hoping that the author would not read the

prescription immediately.

12. 'clutched', 'hit', 'butted': these words show that the author is describing the medical examination as if it were a physical fight.

C. *Find single words or phrases in the passage which have roughly the meanings given below:*

1. described
2. short
3. not new or interesting
4. close friend
5. in a lazy way
6. something that creates extra problems

D. *Match the words under A with the meanings under B. List B has some extra items.*

A	B
1. virulent	(a) made weak by old age or ill health
2. pharmacology	(b) severe; very harmful
3. decrepit	(c) badly formed
4. malignant	(d) illness
5. hamper	(e) lack of hope
6. ailment	(f) difficult to cure
	(g) science of drugs
	(h) primary
	(i) limit

19. Home Country

PETER C. NEWMAN*

But times have changed. The American embassy has long since stopped phoning me; all those great guys are reporting on less benign expressions of our nationalism; and along with that small band of Canadians who were nationalists a decade ago, I find myself a moderate voice in a rising chorus of anti-American sentiment. This attitude seems so foreign to the habitual Canadian cast of mind that it almost amounts to a denial of our national character. After displaying for so long the emotional responses of a fearful, immature twenty-year-old who has not yet resolved his adolescent identity crisis, we are experiencing a mood of surging self-assertion. This new aggressive nationalism is strongest among the radical young and the activist intellectuals, but in the past year it has become an issue that even the old-line liberal internationalists, who still form the country's political establishment, have been unable to avoid. It is as though we have come to realize for the first time the true implications of our dependency on the United States. "Little by little," writes James Eayrs, a University of Toronto professor who has come very lately to the nationalist cause, "our independence is seeping southward. It takes place so painlessly that

---

* **Peter C. Newman (1929～):** Canada의 언론인, 편집인. Renegade in Power등의 저서가 있음

the victim does not notice. But one day he tries to exercise his independence and finds it isn't there—like the decapitated swordsman in the Thurber cartoon who, protesting he's fit to carry on dueling, is told to try and blow his nose."

During the past few years we have been displaying our determination to hold on to our heads in various ways, but nationalism in Canada is still a cause in search of a leader, an issue yet to be joined.

Its historic roots go far deeper than these recent manifestations would suggest. A self-governing colony may sound like a contradiction in terms; yet this has been the underlying theme of our history. Canada moved directly from being a colony of Great Britain to becoming an economic satellite of the United States. Originally, the Canadian nation was a fusion, or rather a living-together, of French-Canadians (following their defeat by the British) and those united Empire Loyalists who left the thirteen colonies after the Revolutionary War because they opted for England and King George. They were joined by waves of Scottish, Irish, and European immigrants fleeing various tyrannies. Born out of many defeats, Canada achieved a form of independence in 1867 (i.e., dominion status within the British Empire), which left its foreign policies to be dictated by Whitehall[1]. Full freedom in international dealings came only in 1931, and it wasn't until 1949 that the judicial committee of the Privy Council[2] in London ceased to be the final appeal from Canadian courts. This prolonged dependence on the mother country caused an impatient generation of Canadian patriots of Lester Pearson's vintage to believe that the umbilical cord with

1. 영국의 주요 관공서가 몰려 있는 London의 거리 이름, 즉 영국 정부
2. 추밀원(영국 왕실의 고문단)

England could be cut only if Canada were aligned with the United States through closer military, economic, and social ties. And so we went directly from being bastard Englishmen to being bastard Americans.

The conquest of the Canadian economy by American businessmen has reduced Canadians to being minority shareholders in their own country. For example, more than 90 percent of all factories in Canada important enough to have at least five thousand names on their payrolls are controlled by parent corporations in the United States. In addition, some 99 percent of oil refining, 85 percent of primary metal smelting, 78 percent of chemical production, and 77 percent of the electrical apparatus industry are American-owned. The cliché is that when the American economy catches a cold, we sneeze; the fact is that we develop pneumonia.

When you point out the extent of American economic domination to Americans living in Canada, they become intensely upset, hurt by our failure to remember that American capital has underwritten most of the country's development risks, reducing from generations to years the time required to attain our high standards of living. They had come to regard Canadians as the dullish denizens of their northernmost "state" and are baffled by all of the recent uproar. What they do not realize, and what it has taken us so long to comprehend, is that in exchange for our borrowed American affluence we have been selling out our way of life. In our naive, northern way, we had no idea that allowing the Americans to develop our natural resources implied we were willing to have them pollute our environment, direct our trade unions, deluge our media, bookstores, magazine racks, movie houses, and even school texts with American ideas and values so that we are in real danger of forgetting who we are and why we are here.

Until recently, any concern with perpetuating the Canadian identity was considered fairly absurd and old-fashioned, since the admired attitude was internationalism and the only real mark of acceptance in every field of endeavor came from the United States. I bought it on Fifth Avenue; he studied at Harvard; she had her hysterectomy at the Mayo; we got our tan in Palm Beach—these were the meaningful accolades. We were the country cousins awed by the new Roman Empire and understood perfectly what Anthony Burgess meant when he wrote: "John Kenneth Galbraith and Marshall McLuhan are the two greatest modern Canadians the United States has produced." All that has changed. The American experience we so envied has become too precious to be entrusted to the new, disturbing America that emerged in the sixties—the America of the Kennedy assassinations, Kent State, and Vietnam.

By the very act of confronting our problems of domination from without and dissension from within, Canadians may be able to rework the miracle of their existence. In any case, having survived for a century as an irrelevant hunk of geography—a kind of gullible Gulliver of the North—we have now joined the mainstream of history at last.

EXERCISES

A. *Answer the following questions.*

1. What does the author say of the foundation of Canada?
2. What impact did the Revolutionary War have on Canada?
3. Why did Canada turn to America?
4. How much is the Canadian economy dependent on America?
5. Can you give other examples of foreign dependency similar

to the situation in Canada?

B. *Fill in the blanks with suitable words.*

1. This attitude almost amounts ( ) a denial of our national character.
2. It ( ) place so painlessly that the victim does not notice.
3. Until recently, any concern ( ) perpetuating the Canadian identity was considered fairly absurd and old-fashioned.
4. The American experience we so envied has become too precious to be entrusted to the new, disturbing America that emerged ( ) the sixties.
5. By the very act of confronting our problems of domination from without and dissension from ( ), Canadians may be able to rework the miracle of their existence.

C. *Choose one of the words that best fits each of the following sentences.*

a. implication	b. international	c. emotional
d. satellite	e. polluted	f. comprehend
g. sentiments	h. generations	i. foreign
j. vintage	k. therapy	

1. The prime minister has condemned this act of terrorism, and the other party leaders have expressed similar ( ).
2. He is a very good person; unkindness is ( ) to his nature.
3. She is an ( ) woman, easily upset by any disturbance.
4. She said very little directly, but a great deal by ( ).

5. The broadcast came from the Great Britain by (   ).
6. The Mafia is an (   ) underworld organization.
7. Prolonged (   ) saves about 80% of the patients of this disease.
8. This has been a (   ) year for the theater in Seoul; so many good plays have been produced.
9. Members of my family have lived in this house for (   ).
10. The child read the story but did not (   ) its full meaning.
11. The river has been (   ) by waste products from the factory.

Dear Mom:

Now that I am a parent of sometimes ungrateful children, I realize I owe you a few apologies.

I'm sorry for every time I said, "I hate you."

I'm sorry for all the times I left the house for school too mad to kiss you good-bye.

I'm sorry for not being brave enough to kiss you in front of my school, instead of down the street, especially when you were nice enough to give me a ride.

I guess what I'm trying to say is I'm sorry for all the things I must have done to hurt your feelings.

Thank you for letting our house be the place where all the neighbor kids were welcome.

Thank you for fixing so many good meals, doing our laundry, and making home a pleasant place to be.

Thank you for all the years you put in to help us grow up to be honest and decent. The list goes on and on.

I love you, Mom.

20. Pain Is Not the Ultimate Enemy

NORMAN COUSINS*

Americans are probably the most pain-conscious people on the face of the earth. For years we have had it drummed into[1] us —in print, on radio, over television, in everyday conversation— that any hint of pain is to be banished as though it were the ultimate evil. As a result, we are becoming a nation of pill-grabbers and hypochondriacs[2], escalating the slightest ache into a searing ordeal.

We know very little about pain and what we don't know makes it hurt all the more. Indeed, no form of illiteracy in the United States is so widespread or costly as ignorance about pain—what it is, what causes it, how to deal with it without panic. Almost everyone can rattle off the names of at least a dozen drugs that can deaden pain from every conceivable cause—all the way from headaches to hemorrhoids[3]. There is far less knowledge about the fact that about 90 percent of pain is self-limiting, that it is not always an indication of poor health, and that, most frequently, it is the result of tension, stress, worry, idleness, boredom, frustration,

---

*** Norman Cousins(1915～):** 미국의 작가, 언론인
1. 자꾸 되풀이하여 심어 주다
2. 건강염려증 환자
3. 치질

suppressed rage, insufficient sleep, overeating, poorly balanced diet, smoking, excessive drinking, inadequate exercise, stale air, or any of the other abuses encountered by the human body in modern society.

The most ignored fact of all about pain is that the best way to eliminate it is to eliminate the abuse. Instead, many people reach almost instinctively for the painkillers—aspirins, barbiturates, codeines, tranquilizers, sleeping pills, and dozens of other analgesics[4] or desensitizing drugs.

Most doctors are profoundly troubled over the extent to which the medical profession today is taking on the trappings of a pain-killing industry. Their offices are overloaded with people who are morbidly but mistakenly convinced that something dreadful is about to happen to them. It is all too evident that the campaign to get people to run to a doctor at the first sign of pain has boomeranged. Physicians find it difficult to give adequate attention to patients genuinely in need of expert diagnosis and treatment because their time is soaked up by people who have nothing wrong with them except a temporary indisposition or a psychogenic ache.

Patients tend to feel indignant and insulted if the physician tells them he can find no organic cause for the pain. They tend to interpret the term "psychogenic" to mean that they are complaining of nonexistent symptoms. They need to be educated about the fact that many forms of pain have no underlying physical cause but are the result, as mentioned earlier, of tension, stress, or hostile factors in the general environment. Sometimes a pain may be a

---

4. 진정제

manifestation of "conversion hysteria[5]"...the name given by Jean Charcot to physical symptoms that have their origins in emotional disturbances.

Obviously, it is folly for an individual to ignore symptoms that could be a warning of a potentially serious illness. Some people are so terrified of getting bad news from a doctor that they allow their malaise to worsen, sometimes past the point of no return. Total neglect is not the answer to hypochondria. The only answer has to be increased education about the way the human body works, so that more people will be able to steer an intelligent course between promiscuous pill-popping and irresponsible disregard of genuine symptoms.

Of all forms of pain, none is more important for the individual to understand than the "threshold" variety. Almost everyone has a telltale ache that is triggered whenever tension or fatigue reaches a certain point. It can take the form of a migraine-type headache or a squeezing pain deep in the abdomen or cramps or a pain in the lower back or even pain in the joints. The individual who has learned how to make the correlation between such threshold pains[6] and their cause doesn't panic when they occur; he or she does something about relieving the stress and tension. Then, if the pain persists despite the absence of apparent cause, the individual will telephone the doctor.

If ignorance about the nature of pain is widespread, ignorance about the way pain-killing drugs work is even more so. What is not generally understood is that many of the vaunted pain-killing drugs conceal the pain without correcting the underlying

5. 전환성 히스테리
6. 통증의 역치

condition. They deaden the mechanism in the body that alerts the brain to the fact that something may be wrong. The body can pay a high price for suppression of pain without regard to its basic cause.

Professional athletes are sometimes severely disadvantaged by trainers whose job it is to keep them in action. The more famous the athlete, the greater the risk that he or she may be subjected to extreme medical measures when injury strikes. The star baseball pitcher whose arm is sore because of a torn muscle or tissue damage may need sustained rest more than anything else. But his team is battling for a place in the World Series; so the trainer or team doctor, called upon to work his magic, reaches for a strong dose of Butazolidine[7] or other powerful pain suppressants. Presto[8], the pain disappears! The pitcher takes his place on the mound and does superbly. That could be the last game, however, in which he is able to throw a ball with full strength. The drugs didn't repair the torn muscle or cause the damaged tissue to heal. What they did was to mask the pain, enabling the pitcher to throw hard, further damaging the torn muscle. Little wonder that so many star athletes are cut down in their prime, more the victims of overzealous treatment of their injuries than of the injuries themselves.

The king of all painkillers, of course, is aspirins. The U. S. Food and Drug Administration permits aspirin to be sold without prescription, but the drug, contrary to popular belief, can be dangerous and, in sustained doses, potentially lethal. Aspirin is self-administered by more people than any other drug in the world.

---

7. 진통제 이름
8. (감탄사) 자!, 빨리!

Some people are aspirin-poppers, taking ten or more a day. What they don't know is that the smallest dose can cause internal bleeding. Even more serious perhaps is the fact that aspirin is antagonistic to collagen[9], which has a key role in the formation of connective tissue. Since many forms of arthritis involve disintegration of the connective tissue, the steady use of aspirin can actually intensify the underlying arthritic condition.

Aspirin is not the only pain-killing drug, of course, that is known to have dangerous side effects. Dr. Daphne A. Roe, of Cornell University, at a medical meeting in New York City in 1974, presented startling evidence of a wide range of hazards associated with sedatives and other pain suppressants. Some of these drugs seriously interfere with the ability of the body to metabolize food properly, producing malnutrition. In some instances, there is also the danger of bone-marrow depression, interfering with the ability of the body to replenish its blood supply.

Pain-killing drugs are among the greatest advances in the history of medicine. Properly used, they can be a boon in alleviating suffering and in treating disease. But their indiscriminate and promiscuous use is making psychological cripples and chronic ailers out of millions of people. The unremitting barrage of advertising for pain-killing drugs, especially over television, has set the stage for a mass anxiety neurosis. Almost from the moment children are old enough to sit upright in front of a television screen, they are being indoctrinated into the hypochondriac's clamorous and morbid world. Little wonder so many people fear pain more than death itself.

It might be a good idea if concerned physicians and educators

---

9. (뼈 따위의) 교원질

could get together to make knowledge about pain an important part of the regular school curriculum. As for the populace at large, perhaps some of the same techniques used by public-service agencies to make people cancer-conscious can be used to counteract the growing terror of pain and illness in general. People ought to know that nothing is more remarkable about the human body than its recuperative drive, given a modicum of respect. If our broadcasting stations cannot provide equal time for responses to the pain-killing advertisements, they might at least set aside a few minutes each day for common-sense remarks on the subject of pain. As for the Food and Drug Administration, it might be interesting to know why an agency that has energetically warned the American people against taking vitamins without prescriptions is doing so little to control over-the-counter[10] sales each year of billions of pain-killing pills, some of which can do more harm than the pain they are supposed to suppress.

SIX WAYS TO MAKE PEOPLE LIKE YOU

1. *Become genuinely interested in other people.*
2. *Smile.*
3. *Remember that a man's name is to him the sweetest and most important sound in any language.*
4. *Be a good listener. Encourage others to talk about themselves.*
5. *Talk in terms of the other man's interest.*
6. *Make the other person feel important — and do it sincerely.*

---

10. (약품이) 의사의 처방 없이도 팔 수 있는

EXERCISES

A. *Answer the following questions.*

1. What is the most widespread form of illiteracy in the United States?
2. What are some of the side effects of pain-killing pills?
3. What is responsible for the wide abuse of pain-killing drugs?
4. What does the author suggest to dissuade people from taking pain-killing drugs?
5. What causes many forms of pain which have no underlying physical causes?

B. *Fill in the blanks with suitable words.*

1. Americans are probably the most pain-conscious people (   ) the face of the earth.
2. For years we have had it drummed (   ) us that any hint of pain is to be banished as though it were the ultimate evil.
3. Almost everyone can rattle (   ) the names of at least a dozen drugs.
4. The most ignored fact of all about pain is that the best way to eliminate it is (   ) eliminate the abuse.
5. Instead, many people reach almost instinctively (   ) the painkillers.
6. The offices are overloaded with people who are morbidly but mistakenly convinced that something dreadful is (   ) to happen to them.
7. Their time is soaked (   ) by people who have nothing wrong with them except a temporary indisposition or a psychogenic ache.

8. Patients tend to feel indignant if the physician tells them he can find no organic cause (   ) the pain.
9. They tend to interpret the term "psychogenic" to mean that they are complaining (   ) nonexistent symptoms.
10. Of all forms of pain, none is (   ) important for the individual to understand than the "threshold" variety.
11. The individual who has learned how to make the correlation (   ) such threshold pains and their cause doesn't panic when they occur.
12. Professional athletes are sometimes severely disadvantaged by trainers whose job (   ) is to keep them in action.
13. The star baseball pitcher whose arm is sore because of a torn muscle or tissue damage may need sustained rest more than anything (   ).
14. That could be the last game, however, in which he is able to throw a ball (   ) full strength.
15. What they don't know is (   ) the smallest dose can cause internal bleeding.
16. Aspirin is not the only pain-killing drug, of course, that is known (   ) have dangerous side effects.
17. As for the populace (   ) large, the same techniques can be used to counteract the growing terror of pain and illness in general.
18. People ought to know that nothing is more remarkable about the human body than its recuperative drive, (   ) a modicum of respect.
19. It might be interesting to know why the agency is doing so little to control over-the-counter sales each year of billions of pain-killing pills, some of which can (   ) more harm than the pain they are supposed to suppress.

C. *Choose one of the words that best fits each of the following sentences.*

a. mechanism	b. insult	c. potentially
d. ignorance	e. lethal	f. underlying
g. indication	h. boomeranged	i. malaise
j. symptoms	k. nonexistent	

1. The students were kept in complete ( ) of the college's financial situation.
2. Can you give me any ( ) of how I did in the English test?
3. Her plan to reduce the number of workers ( ) on her, and she lost her own job.
4. You will ( ) her if you don't go to her birthday party.
5. Their government is bankrupt, and public services are now practically ( ).
6. The ( ) message of the report was quite optimistic.
7. The ( ) don't appear until a few days after you are infected.
8. He is ( ) our best golf player, but he needs to practise much harder.
9. The underlying social ( ) in this country is causing a steady decline in production and trade.
10. The clock doesn't go; there's something wrong with the ( ).
11. Even a bat can be a ( ) weapon in some cases.

21. The Values of Europe

HAROLD NICOLSON*

I have often in the course of my life lived outside Europe. I have lived in Russia, in Turkey, in Persia, and in the United States. However great may have been the interest and instruction which these countries provided, however lavish may have been the hospitality and the friendliness that their inhabitants showed me, I was often conscious of the aching tooth of homesickness. When I analysed that homesickness I realized that it was different from the accustomed yearning for one's own family and friends, for one's own rooms and books, or for the familiar outlook upon garden and woods. It was wider than this, arising from a sense of strangeness at being plunged into an alien civilization and a constant desire to find myself back again behind the ancient parapets[1] of Europe and in a cultural atmosphere which I understood and loved. So acute and so recurrent did this homesickness become that I was struck by the fact that European associations assumed for me an importance which was really disproportionate.

At Chicago once, when attending some reception of a literary society, I was introduced to a young Frenchman who was over

---

* **Harold Nicolson(1886~1968):** 영국의 외교관, 전기 작가, 언론인, 비평가. Sweet Waters(1921)등의 작품이 있음

1. frontiers

there studying at the university. I have met many young Frenchmen in my life and have no reason to suppose that this particular specimen was in any way exceptional; yet I felt for him a sudden familiarity which my American friends failed to inspire. I am sure that the Americans who surrounded us were more charming, more gifted, more cultured than we were, but they lacked something possessed by that rather insignificant little spectacled student: they lacked the European tradition. Often, when I have returned from across the Atlantic or from the East or South have the lights of the Lizard or Finisterre or Ushant[2] appeared to blink at me with a special welcome. If, after months spent in the New World or the East, I land at Cherbourg or Marseilles, the small white farms of Normandy[3] or the olives of Provence[4] seem to me as intimate and understandable as are the pavements of Piccadilly or the orchards of Kent[5].

These are but incidental illustrations and might seem to indicate no more than that man is by nature a sedentary[6] animal and that when he returns from his wanderings he welcomes the familiar with comfortable ease. Yet that is not exactly the point. The point is that when I am outside Europe, however congenial may be my surroundings, I feel more or less of an alien; and that when I return to Europe I feel immediately at home. Yet, why, when living for three years in Turkey and Persia, living in my own house with my own servants, surrounded by friends and interests, should I be unable

---

2. 각각 England 서남부의 반도, Spain 서북부의 갑(岬), 그리고 France 서북 해안에 있는 섬
3. Cherbourg항을 포함하는 France북부 지방
4. Marseilles항구를 포함하는 France 남부지방
5. England남동부 지방
6. 이주하지 않는

to divest[7] myself of the feeling of not-belonging? Why, after months living with esteemed and kindly friends in the United States, should I again and again be assailed by the thought that there is something missing? Why, when I land at Brindisi or Marseilles, which superficially are far more alien to me than Massachusetts or Illinois, should I feel that I have recovered my identity? It is because I have again found myself within a civilization formed and conditioned by traditions that I understand and share. In other words, I have recovered my European values.

Before I consider these values I should say something about the expression 'Europe'. I sometimes feel that what I mean by 'Europe'—by that special area of the earth's surface which gives me the feeling of recognition and familiarity—is not identical with what is marked Europe on the maps. It has often seemed to me that the eastern fringes of my continent are not to an equal extent the inheritors of our special values. I have never, for instance, regarded Russia, even when I visited it before the first world war, as a true inheritor of the European tradition, and I agreed with those who used to say that Asia began on the east bank of the Niemen[8]. I have often felt that the western half of Germany was more European than its eastern marches[9] and I have been tempted to credit the theory that a difference exists between those areas of Europe that experienced the long discipline of Roman occupation and those which lay beyond the frontier of the Roman Empire.

According to this theory one of the most disastrous battles in history was the catastrophe inflicted on Varus[10] and his legions[11]

7. 제거하다
8. Russia 와 Poland사이의 강
9. 두 나라 사이의 경계 지방
10. 9세기에 독일에서 패한 로마 장군

by the central tribes of Germany, a defeat that induced the aging Augustus to withdraw the Roman frontier from the Elbe to the Rhine. Even today one can detect a certain difference in the culture between those European tribes who for centuries enjoyed the benefits of Roman imperialism and those who remained beyond the mighty rampart[12] of law and order in a comparatively savage state.

On this assumption (and I am aware that it can well become an exaggerated assumption), the first formative influence that went to mould the values of Europe was Roman colonialism. The rule of the Romans was not tyrannical; their principle was, in the words of Virgil, 'to spare the submissive but to crush the proud'; they brought great practical benefits—such as cities, roads and commerce—to the conquered barbarians, but the greatest benefits that they accorded or imposed were peace, order, and the rule of law. During the centuries of their dominance they taught uncivilized tribes that order was preferable to anarchy, and that the individual could achieve more valuable opportunities for happiness and self-expression in a society subject to certain known rules than in one governed merely by the principles of might being right.

This lesson, although often forgotten, became endemic[13] and therefore recurrent; in the turbulent centuries that followed the withdrawal of the Roman legions it engendered the principle that the rule of law was preferable to arbitrary despotism and as such it led, not merely to famous enactments such as Magna Carta[14], but

---

11. 약 3,000명의 군인으로 구성되는 로마 군단
12. 성벽
13. 한 지방 특유의, 풍토성의
14. 대헌장,Magna Carta; the great charter of English personal and political liberty obtained from King John in A.D. 1215

to a habit—a habit of common thought regarding the proper relation between the community and the individual. Admittedly this theory or doctrine has since then been adopted by communities who never experienced a Roman conquest and in many instances has been applied by them with even greater logic, vigour, or consistency. Yet younger societies have received the doctrine so to speak second-hand and ready-made; they do not share our European memory of the long and bitter struggles through which the idea triumphed. The memory of such struggles has a value of its own.

One of the significant distinctions between the old European world on the one hand, and on the other the New World of the West and the mighty other world that is forming and creating itself between the Russian frontier and the China Seas, is the consciousness of tradition. In younger, and it may be more dynamic, societies, such words as `tradition' and 'traditionalism' are used as it were contemptuously: with us they are associated with the unconscious memory of many centuries of effort. The Englishman, the Frenchman, the German, the Italian, and the Spaniard, even if he be ignorant of the details of his history, is aware that it stretches back into the mists of a palaeolithic[15] epoch, and has been marked by much failure, innumerable mistakes, constant struggle, occasional triumphs and many disasters. Other civilizations, such as the Indian and the Chinese, have behind them an even older tradition. Yet their traditions have proved comparatively static; ours have been constantly dynamic. The variation in our ambition, impulses, prejudices and affections has given us a certain sense of relativity, a certain acceptance of the fact that the conventions and watch-words of one generation may prove

---

15. 구석기 시대의

irrelevant to the needs of the generations that follow. This has produced in us old Europeans the habit of inductive rather than deductive reasoning and with it, not scepticism exactly, not exactly opportunism, but a mood of tolerance. One of the values of Europe, therefore, is that, unlike other societies, we are never absolutely positive that the other man is utterly wrong whereas we are utterly right. In this manner tradition with us has an elastic rather than a rigid effect: I call that a great value.

Inheriting as we do the massive administrative and legal orderliness of the Romans we also, although more indirectly, inherit the Greek admiration for abstract ideas and their distrust of material success. I am not suggesting that the European business man is more inclined than is the American business man or the Australian business man to devote hours of rumination[16] to the nature of the beautiful and the good. But I do suggest that among the many tributaries that have gone to swell the mighty river of European civilization a clear spring of Attic[17] water still trickles through the centuries and inclines us to doubt whether money is after all the most important thing on earth. The religious controversies which, until the end of the seventeenth century, caused such atrocious—and to our modern minds unnecessary—suffering in Europe, were accompanied by great spiritual vigour and selflessness. These experiences, atrocious though they often were, have led today not merely to a wider tolerance but to a living conviction that man does not live by bread alone. Undeniably this conviction is shared and practised by other civilizations; but we in Europe have acquired it through centuries of trial and error and it is embedded as a warning

---

16. 숙고, 묵상
17. 아테네의

in our memories. We have learnt that fanaticism is always limiting and may become cruel.

I am not saying that the six great values that I have mentioned are not present in other societies. I am saying only that we acquired them by experience whereas others have acquired them by precept. Our fight for freedom has not been concentrated into an episode. It has been gradual in space and time. Our faith in law, our belief in tradition, our habit of tolerance, our empiricism, our distrust of material standards, have after centuries of trial and error become natural to us. It is not that our faiths and ideas are better than those of other peoples; it is that they are more mature. And, of all European values, the greatest is maturity.

EXERCISES

A. *Answer the following questions.*

1. What was the writer conscious of when he lived outside Europe?
2. What was the first influence that moulded the values of Europe?
3. What was the greatest legacy bequeathed by the Romans to the tribes they conquered?
4. What distinction does the writer draw between the traditions of Europe and the older traditions of India and China?
5. What has Europe inherited from the Greeks?
6. What did the religious wars of the 16th and 17th centuries contribute to the values of modern Europe?
7. What are the six great values mentioned by the writer at the

end of the essay?

B. *Consider the following phrases, and then insert them in the blank spaces in the sentences below.*

a. to an extent	b. the point is that
c. not that	d. in the course of
e. such as	f. not merely
g. so to speak	h. on the other hand
i. according to	j. for instance
k. no more than	l. more or less

1. The enemy should be defeated ( ) the year.
2. He has ( ) two sons to share his fortune.
3. ( ) you must do your best in what you do.
4. She seemed ( ) familiar with the subject.
5. They lacked vitality ( ) that was surprising.
6. You can't rely on her: ( ), she arrived an hour late for an important meeting yesterday.
7. ( ) our records, the books you have borrowed should now be returned to the library.
8. A plan ( ) you propose will never succeed.
9. You are, ( ), a fish out of water.
10. I know this job of mine isn't well paid, but ( ) I don't have to work long hours.
11. She was ( ) beautiful, but talented.
12. ( ) I dislike the task, but that I am not equal to it.

C. *Rewrite the following sentences without the participial construction, but giving exactly the same meaning.*

(e.g.) The twins were always sick when flying in an airplane.
The twins were always sick when they flew in an airplane.

1. While ordering the meal he whispered something to the head waiter.

2. Having no relations he bequeathed all his money to charity.

3. Before going abroad he obtained a visa for Poland.

4. Having spent all his life in the East my uncle found that he couldn't manage without servants.

5. After reading the book she sent a letter of congratulations to the author.

6. After landing in Nice he took the train to Paris.

7. Not being rich he decided against buying a motor-car.

8. The new Congressman made a good impression when making his maiden speech.

9. He became very impatient through having to lie in bed with a broken leg.

10. On hearing the criticisms of his opera the composer agreed to revise it.

22. The Electronic Cottage

ALVIN TOFFLER*

Hidden inside our advance to a new production system is a potential for social change so breathtaking in scope that few among us have been willing to face its meaning. For we are about to revolutionize our homes as well.

Apart from encouraging smaller work units, apart from permitting a decentralization and de-urbanization of production, apart from altering the actual character of work, the new production system could shift literally millions of jobs out of the factories and offices into which the Second Wave[1] swept them and right back where they came from originally: the home. If this were to happen, every institution we know, from the family to the school and the corporation, would be transformed.

Watching masses of peasants scything a field three hundred years ago, only a madman would have dreamed that the time would soon come when the fields would be depopulated, when people would crowd into urban factories to earn their daily bread. And only a madman would have been right. Today it takes an act

---

* **Alvin Toffler(1928～　):** 독일에서 대학을 마치고 뒤에 미국에 정착한 미래학 학자. Future Shock(1970), The Third Wave(1980)등의 저서가 있음

1. 약 300년 전에 일어난 산업혁명을 말함. 제 3의 물결은 Toffler가 그의 책 The Third Wave(1980)에서 말한 Electronics 혁명에 의한 고도의 기술 시대를 뜻함

of courage to suggest that our biggest factories and office towers may, within our lifetimes, stand half-empty, reduced to use as ghostly warehouses or converted into living space. Yet this is precisely what the new mode of production makes possible: a return to cottage industry on a new, higher, electronic basis, and with it a new emphasis on the home as the center of society.

To suggest that millions of us may soon spend our time at home, instead of going out to an office or factory, is to unleash an immediate shower of objections. And there are many sensible reasons for skepticism. 'People don't want to work at home, even if they could. Look at all the women struggling to get out of the home and into a job!' 'How can you get any work done with kids running around?' 'People won't be motivated unless there's a boss watching them.' 'People need face-to-face contact with each other to develop the trust and confidence necessary to work together.' 'The architecture of the average home isn't set up for it.' 'What do you mean work at home—a small blast furnace in every basement?' 'What about zoning restrictions and landlords who object?' 'The unions will kill the idea.' 'How about the tax collector? The tax people are getting tougher on deductions claimed for working at home.' And the ultimate stopper: 'What, and stay home all with my wife (or husband)?

Even old Karl Marx would have frowned. Working at home, he believed, was a reactionary form of production because 'the agglomeration in one workshop' was 'a necessary condition for the division of labor in society'. In short, there were, and are, many reasons (and pseudoreasons) for regarding the whole idea as silly.

Yet there were equally, if not more, compelling reasons three hundred years ago to believe people would never move *out* of the home and field to work in factories. After all, they had labored in their own cottages and the nearby land for 10,000 years, not a mere 300. The entire structure of family life, the process of childbearing and personality formation, the whole system of property and power, the culture, the daily struggle for existence were all bound to the hearth and the soil by a thousand invisible chains. Yet these chains were slashed in short order[2] as soon as a new system of production appeared.

Today that is happening again, and a whole group of social and economic forces are converging to transfer the locus of work.

To begin with, the shift from Second Wave manufacturing to the new, more advanced Third Wave manufacturing reduces, as we just saw, the number of workers who actually have to manipulate physical goods. This means that even in the manufacturing sector an increasing amount of work is being done that—given the right configuration of telecommunications and other equipment—could be accomplished anywhere, including one's own living-room. Nor is this just a science fiction fantasy.

When Western Electric shifted from producing electromechanical switching equipment for the phone company to making electronic switching gear, the work force at its advanced manufacturing facility in Northern Illinois was transformed. Before the changeover, production workers outnumbered white-collar and technical workers three to one. Today the ratio is one to one. This means that fully half of the 2,000 workers now handle information instead of things, and much of their work can be done at home. Don Cuomo, director of engineering at the Northern Illinois facility put it flatly: 'If you include engineers, ten to twenty-five per cent of what is done here could be done at home with existing

2. 즉각, 지체 없이

technology.'

Cuomo's manager of engineering, Gerald Mitchell, went even further. 'All told,' he stated, '600 to 700 of the 2,000 could *now*—with existing technology—work at home. And in five years, we could go far beyond that.'

These informed 'guesstimates' are remarkably similar to those made by Dar Howard, manufacturing manager of the Hewlett-Packard factory in Colorado Springs: 'We have 1,000 in actual manufacturing. Technologically, maybe 250 of them could work at home. The logistics would be complicated but the tooling and capital equipment would not prevent it. In white-collar research and development, if you're willing to invest in [computer] terminals, one half to three quarters could also work at home.' At Hewlett-Packard that would add up to an additional 350 to 520 workers.

If significant numbers of employees in the manufacturing sector could be shifted to the home even now, then it is safe to say that a considerable slice of the white-collar sector—where there are no materials to handle—could also make that transition.

Indeed, an unmeasured but appreciable amount of work is already being done at home by such people as salesmen and saleswomen who work by phone or visit, and only occasionally touch base at the office; by architects and designers; by a burgeoning pool of specialized consultants in many industries; by large numbers of human-service workers like therapists or psychologists; by music teachers and language instructors; by art dealer, investment counselors, insurance agents, lawyers, and academic researchers; and by many other categories of white-collar, technical, and professional people.

These are, moreover, among the most rapidly expanding work

classifications, and when we suddenly make available technologies that can place a low-cost 'work station[3]' in any home, providing it with a 'smart' typewriter, perhaps, along with a facsimile machine or computer console and teleconferencing equipment, the possibilities for home work are radically extended.

Children, meanwhile, would also be likely to grow up differently in the electronic cottage, if for no other reason than that they would actually see work taking place. First Wave children, from their first blink of consciousness, saw their parents at work. Second Wave children, by contrast—at least in recent generations—were segregated in schools and divorced from real work life. Most today have only the foggiest notion of what their parents do or how they live while at work.

The fact is that children today—especially affluent children—are totally divorced from one of the most important dimensions of their parents' lives. In an electronic cottage kids not only observe work, they may, after a certain age, engage in it themselves. Second Wave restrictions on child labor—originally well-intentioned and necessary, but now largely an anachronistic device to keep young people out of the crowded job market—become more difficult to enforce in the home setting. Certain forms of work, indeed, might be specifically designed for youngsters and even integrated with their education.

The alienation of youth today flows in large measure from being forced to accept a nonproductive role in society during an endlessly prolonged adolescence. The electronic cottage would counteract this situation.

Unions (and teachers, whether unionized or not) will lobby for

3. 책상 딸린 사무실에서 한 사람이 일할 수 있는 면적(구역)

ever-longer years of compulsory or near-compulsory schooling. To the extent that they succeed, millions of young people will continue to be forced into the painful limbo of prolonged adolescence. We may, therefore, see a sharp contrast between young people who grow up fast because of early work responsibilities in the electronic cottage and those who mature more slowly outside.

Over the long pull[4], however, we can expect education also to change. More learning will occur outside, rather than inside, the classroom. Despite the pressure from unions, the years of compulsory schooling will grow shorter, not longer. Instead of rigid age segregation, young and old will mingle. Education will become more interspersed and interwoven with work, and more spread out over a lifetime. And work itself—whether production for the market or prosumption[5] for use in the home—will probably begin earlier in life than it has in the last generation or two. For just such reasons, Third Wave civilization may well favor quite different traits among the young—less responsiveness to peers, less consumption-orientation, and less hedonistic self-involvement.

Whether this is so or not, one thing is certain. Growing up will be different. And so will the resultant personalities.

As the adolescent matures and enters the job arena, new forces come into play on his or her personality, rewarding some traits and punishing or penalizing others.

Throughout the Second Wave era, work in the factories and offices steadily grew more repetitive, specialized, and time-pressured, and employers wanted workers who were obedient,

---

4. In the long run, in the end
5. production + consumption의 합성어

punctual, and willing to perform rote tasks. The corresponding traits were fostered by the schools and rewarded by the corporation.

As the Third Wave cuts across our society, work grows less, not more, repetitive. It becomes less fragmented, with each person doing a somewhat larger, rather than smaller, task. Flexitime[6] and self-pacing replace the old need for mass synchronization of behavior. Workers are forced to cope with more frequent changes in their tasks, as well as a blinding succession of personnel transfers, product changes, and reorganizations.

What Third Wave employers increasingly need, therefore, are men and women who accept responsibility, who understand how their work dovetails with that of others, who can handle ever larger tasks, who adapt swiftly to changed circumstances, and who are sensitively tuned in[7] to the people around them.

The Second Wave firm frequently paid off for plodding bureaucratic behavior. The Third Wave firm requires people who are less pre-programmed and faster on their feet. The difference, says Donald Conover, general manager of Corporate Education for Western Electric, is like that between classical musicians who play each note according to a predetermined, pre-set pattern, and jazz improvisers who, once having decided what song to play, sensitively pick up cues from one another and, on the basis of that, decide what notes to play next.

Such people are complex, individualistic, proud of the ways in which they differ from other people. They typify the demassified work force needed by Third Wave industry.

---

6. 근무시간의 자유선택제
7. 맞추다, 조화시키다

EXERCISES

A. *Answer the following questions.*

1. What is cottage industry?
2. What is happening to the number of production workers and that of white-collar and technical workers?
3. What are the characteristics of the Third Wave manufacturing?
4. How will the electronic cottage affect the children?
5. How will flexitime and self-pacing affect the production of goods?
6. What impact does the Third Wave have on education?
7. What are the major differences between the Second Wave and the Third Wave?

B. *Fill in the blanks with suitable words.*

1. The new production system could shift literally millions of jobs out of the factories and offices (　　) which the Second Wave swept them.
2. If this (　　) to happen, every institution we know, from the family to the school and the corporation, would be transformed.
3. People would crowd into urban factories to (　　) their daily bread.
4. Today it (　　) an act of courage to suggest that our biggest factories and office towers may stand half-empty.
5. At Hewlett-Packard that would add (　　) to an additional 350 to 520 workers.
6. Children would also be likely to grow up differently in the electronic cottage, if (　　) no other reason than that they

would actually see work taking place.

7. Second Wave children were segregated in schools and divorced ( ) real work life.
8. Certain forms of work, indeed, might be specifically designed for youngsters and even integrated ( ) their education.
9. We may see a sharp contrast between young people who grow up fast because of early work responsibilities in the electronic cottage and those who mature more ( ) outside.
10. As the adolescent matures and enters the job arena, new forces come ( ) play on his or her personality, rewarding some traits and punishing or penalizing others.
11. The Second Wave firm frequently paid ( ) for plodding bureaucratic behavior.

C. *Give the correct forms of the words given in the brackets.*

1. Look at all the women (struggle) to get out of the home and into a job.
2. The (alien) of youth today flows from being forced to accept a nonproductive role in society during an endlessly prolonged adolescence.
3. Throughout the Second Wave era, work in the factories and offices steadily grew more (repeat).
4. Workers are forced to cope with more frequent changes in their tasks, as well as a (blind) succession of personnel transfers and reorganizations.
5. They (type) the demassified work force needed by Third Wave industry.

D. *Choose one of the words that best fits each of the following sentences.*

a. informed	b. done	c. flatly
d. outnumbered	e. claimed	f. unleashed
g. watching	h. literally	

1. The Olympic Games were watched by (   ) billions of people around the world.
2. The enemy bombers (   ) a terrible attack on the city.
3. How can you get any work (   ) with kids running around?
4. People won't be motivated unless there's a boss (   ) them.
5. The tax people are getting tougher on deductions (   ) for working at home.
6. The government troops were completely (   ) by the enemy.
7. She (   ) refused to give us any information about the latest development of the war.
8. Please keep me (   ) of any developments in the situation.

A boat that stays in the harbor never encounters danger — but it also never gets anywhere.

23. A Modest Proposal

for Preventing the Children of Ireland from Being a Burden to Their Parents or Country

JONATHAN SWIFT*

It is a melancholy object to those who walk through this great town[1], or travel in the country, when they see the streets, the roads, and cabin-doors, crowded with beggars of the female sex, followed by three, four, or six children, all in rags, and importuning every passenger for an alms. These mothers, instead of being able to work for their honest livelihood, are forced to employ all their time in strolling to beg sustenance for their helpless infants; who, as they grow up, either turn thieves for want of work, or leave their dear native country to fight for the Pretender in Spain, or sell themselves to the Barbadoes[2].

I think it is agreed by all parties, that this prodigious number of children in the arms, or on the backs, or at the heels of their

---

* **Jonathan Swift(1667~1745):** Ireland의 풍자 소설가 및 시인. Dublin태생. 한동안 정치에 몸 담았다가 후에 영국의 억압에 항거하여 Irish 국민의 전사가 되다. Gulliver's Travels, A Tale of a Tube등의 작품이 있음

1. Dublin
2. 많은 가난한 Ireland인들이 가난을 피해 Barbadoes와 다른 영국 식민지로 이주 함. King James II가 실각하고 왕위를 주장하는 그의 아들인 Pretender가 France, Spain등지에서 망명생할을 하며 왕위 탈환을 노릴 때 많은 Irish인들이 그에게 가담했음

mothers, and frequently of their fathers, is, in the present deplorable state of the kingdom, a very great additional grievance; and, therefore, whoever could find out a fair, cheap, and easy method of making these children sound, useful members of the commonwealth, would deserve so well of the public, as to have his statue set up for a preserver of the nation.

But my intention is very far from being confined to provide only for the children of professed beggars; it is of a much greater extent, and shall take in the whole number of infants at a certain age, who are born of parents in effect as little able to support them, as those who demand our charity in the streets.

As to my own part, having turned my thoughts for many years upon this important subject, and maturely weighed the several schemes of our projectors[3], I have always found them grossly mistaken in their computation. It is true, a child just dropped from its dam[4] may be supported by her milk for a solar year, with little other nourishment; at most not above the value of two shillings, which the mother may certainly get, or the value in scraps, by her lawful occupation of begging; and it is exactly at one year old that I propose to provide for them in such a manner as instead of being a charge upon their parents or the parish, or wanting food and raiment for the rest of their lives, they shall, on the contrary, contribute to the feeding and partly to the clothing, of many thousands.

There is likewise another great advantage in my scheme, that it will prevent those voluntary abortions, and that horrid practice of women murdering their bastard children, alas, too frequent among

---

3. 위대한 사상을 생각해 내는 사람
4. (네발 짐승) 새끼를 낳다

us, sacrificing the poor innocent babes, I doubt, more to avoid the expense than the shame, which would move tears and pity in the most savage and inhuman breast.

The number of souls in this kingdom[5] being usually reckoned one million and a half, of these I calculate there may be about two hundred thousand couples whose wives are breeders; from which number I subtract thirty thousand couples, who are able to maintain their own children, (although I apprehend there cannot be so many, under the present distresses of the kingdom;) but this being granted, there will remain a hundred and seventy thousand breeders. I again subtract fifty thousand, for those women who miscarry, or whose children die by accident or disease within the year. There only remain a hundred and twenty thousand children of poor parents annually born. The question therefore is, how this number shall be reared and provided for, which, as I have already said, under the present situation of affairs, is utterly impossible by all the methods hitherto proposed. For we can neither employ them in handicraft or agriculture; we neither build houses (I mean in the country) nor cultivate land: they can very seldom pick up a livelihood by stealing, till they arrive at six years old, except where they are of towardly[6] parts[7]; although I confess they learn the rudiments much earlier; during which time they can, however, be properly looked upon only as probationers; as I have been informed by a principal gentleman in the county of Cavan, who protested to me, that he never knew above one or two instances under the age of six, even in a part of the kingdom so renowned for

5. Ireland
6. dutiful, tractable
7. 소질, 천성

the quickest proficiency in that art.

I am assured by our merchants, that a boy or a girl before twelve years old is no salable commodity; and even when they come to this age they will not yield above three pounds, or three pounds and half-a-crown at most, on the exchange; which cannot turn to account[8] either to the parents or kingdom, the charge of nutriment and rags having been at least four times that value.

I shall now, therefore, humbly propose my own thoughts, which I hope will not be liable to the least objection.

I have been assured by a very knowing American of my acquaintance in London, that a young healthy child, well nursed, is, at a year old, a most delicious, nourishing, and wholesome food, whether stewed, roasted, baked, or boiled; and I make no doubt that it will equally serve in a fricassee or a ragout[9].

I do therefore humbly offer it to public consideration that of the hundred and twenty thousand children already computed, twenty thousand may be reserved for breed, whereof only one-fourth part to be males; which is more than we allow to sheep, black-cattle, or swine, and my reason is, that these children are seldom the fruits of marriage, a circumstance not much regarded by our savages, therefore one male will be sufficient to serve four females. That the remaining hundred thousand may, at a year old, be offered in sale to the persons of quality and fortune through the kingdom; always advising the mother to let them suck plentifully in the last month, so as to render them plump and fat for a good table. A child will make two dishes at an entertainment for friends; and when the family dines alone, the fore or hind quarter

8. 보탬이 되다
9. highly seasoned meat stew

will make a reasonable dish, and, seasoned with a little pepper or salt, will be very good boiled on the fourth day, especially in winter.

I have reckoned upon a medium that a child just born will weigh twelve pounds, and in a solar year, if tolerably nursed, will increase to twenty-eight pounds.

I grant this food will be somewhat dear, and therefore very proper for landlords, who, as they have already devoured most of the parents, seem to have the best title to the children.

Infant's flesh will be in season throughout the year, but more plentifully in March, and a little before and after: for we are told by a grave author, an eminent French physician[10], that fish being a prolific diet, there are more children born in Roman Catholic countries about nine months after Lent, than at any other season; therefore, reckoning a year after Lent, the markets will be more glutted than usual, because the number of Popish infants is at least three to one in this kingdom; and therefore it will have one other collateral advantage, by lessening the Papists among us.

I have already computed the charge of nursing a beggar's child (in which list I reckon all cottagers, labourers, and four-fifths of the farmers) to be about two shillings per annum, rags included; and I believe no gentleman would repine to give ten shillings for the carcass of a good fat child, which, as I have said, will make four dishes of excellent nutritive meat, when he has only some particular friend, or his own family, to dine with him. Thus the squire will learn to be a good landlord, and grow popular among his tenants; the mother will have eight shillings net profit, and be fit for work till she produces another child.

10. 프랑스의 풍자가 Rabelais

Those who are more thrifty (as I must confess the times require) may flay the carcass; the skin of which, artificially[11] dressed, will make admirable gloves for ladies, and summer-boots for fine gentlemen.

As to our city of Dublin, shambles[12] may be appointed for this purpose in the most convenient parts of it, and butchers, we may be assured, will not be wanting; although I rather recommend buying the children alive, then dressing them hot from the knife, as we do roasting pigs.

A very worthy person, a true lover of his country, and whose virtues I highly esteem, was lately pleased, in discoursing on this matter, to offer a refinement upon my scheme. He said, that many gentlemen of this kingdom, having of late destroyed their deer, he conceived that the want of venison[13] might be well supplied by the bodies of young lads and maidens, not exceeding fourteen years of age, nor under twelve; so great a number of both sexes in every country being now ready to starve for want of work and service; and these to be disposed of by their parents, if alive, or otherwise by their nearest relations. But, with due deference to so excellent a friend, and so deserving a patriot, I cannot be altogether in his sentiments; for as to the males, my American acquaintance assured me, from frequent experience, that their flesh was generally tough and lean, like that of our schoolboys, by continual exercise, and their taste disagreeable; and to fatten them would not answer the charge. Then as to the females, it would, I think, with humble submission, be a loss to the public, because

11. skillfully
12. slaughterhouses
13. 사냥해서 잡은 고기

they soon would become breeders themselves: and besides, it is not improbable that some scrupulous[14] people might be apt to censure such a practice, (although indeed very unjustly,) as a little bordering upon cruelty; which, I confess, has always been with me the strongest objection against any project, how well soever intended.

But in order to justify my friend, he confessed that this expedient was put into his head by the famous Psalmanazar[15], a native of the island Formosa, who came from thence to London above twenty years ago; and in conversation told my friend, that in his country, when any young person happened to be put to death, the executioner sold the carcass to persons of quality as a prime dainty; and that in his time the body of a plump girl of fifteen, who was crucified for an attempt to poison the emperor, was sold to his imperial majesty's prime minister of state, and other great mandarins of the court, in joints from the gibbet, at four hundred crowns. Neither indeed can I deny, that, if the same use were made of several plump young girls in this town, who, without one single groat[16] to their fortunes, cannot stir abroad without a chair[17], and appear at playhouse and assemblies in foreign fineries which they never will pay for, the kingdom would not be the worse.

Some persons of desponding spirit are in great concern about that vast number of poor people, who are aged, diseased, or maimed; and I have been desired to employ my thoughts, what

14. 인정에 약한
15. George Psalmanazar(1679~1763): 유명한 사기꾼. 영국 주교, 귀족, 대만 과학자 로 사칭
16. 4 pence, 작은 금액
17. sedan chair

course may be taken to ease the nation of so grievous an encumbrance. But I am not in the least pain upon that matter, because it is very well known, that they are every day dying, and rotting, by cold and famine, and filth and vermin, as fast as can be reasonably expected. And as to the young labourers, they are now in almost as hopeful a condition: they cannot get work, and consequently pine[18] away for want of nourishment, to a degree, that if at any time they are accidentally hired to common labour, they have not strength to perform it; and thus the country and themselves are happily delivered from the evils to come.

I have too long digressed, and therefore shall return to my subject. I think the advantages by the proposal which I have made are obvious and many, as well as of the highest importance.

For first, as I have already observed, it would greatly lessen the number of Papists, with whom we are yearly over-run, being the principal breeders of the nation, as well as our most dangerous enemies; and who stay at home on purpose to deliver the kingdom to the Pretender, hoping to take their advantage by the absence of so many good Protestants, who have chosen rather to leave their country than stay at home and pay tithes against their conscience to an Episcopal curate.

Secondly, the poorer tenants will have something valuable of their own, which by law may be made liable to distress[19], and help to pay their landlord's rent; their corn and cattle being already seized, and money a thing unknown.

Thirdly, whereas the maintenance of a hundred thousand children, from two years old and upwards, cannot be computed at

18. 수척해지다
19. distraint, (법률) 압류

less than ten shillings a piece per annum, the nation's stock will be thereby increased fifty thousand pounds per annum, beside the profit of a new dish introduced to the tables of all gentlemen of fortune in the kingdom, who have any refinement in taste. And the money will circulate among ourselves, the goods being entirely of our own growth and manufacture.

Fourthly, the constant breeders, beside the gain of eight shillings sterling per annum by the sale of their children, will be rid of the charge of maintaining them after the first year.

Fifthly, this food would likewise bring great custom to taverns; where the vintners will certainly be so prudent as to procure the best receipts[20] for dressing it to perfection, and, consequently, have their houses frequented by all the fine gentlemen, who justly value themselves upon their knowledge in good eating: and a skillful cook, who understands how to oblige his guests, will contrive to make it as expensive as they please.

Sixthly, this would be great inducement to marriage, which all wise nations have either encouraged by rewards, or enforced by laws and penalties. It would increase the care and tenderness of mothers toward their children, when they were sure of a settlement for life to the poor babes, provided in some sort by the public, to their annual profit instead of expense. We should see an honest emulation among the married women, which of them could bring the fattest child to the market. Men would become as fond of their wives during the time of their pregnancy as they are now of their mares in foal, their cows in calf, their sows when they are ready to farrow; nor offer to beat or kick them (as is too frequent a practice) for fear of a miscarriage.

---

20. 요리법

Many other advantages might be enumerated. For instance, the addition of some thousand carcasses in our exportation of barrelled beef; the propagation of swine's flesh, and improvement in the art of making good bacon, so much wanted among us by the great destruction of pigs, too frequent at our table; which are no way comparable in taste or magnificence to a well-grown, fat, yearling child, which, roasted whole, will make a considerable figure at a lord mayor's feast, or any other public entertainment. But this, and many others, I omit, being studious of brevity.

Supposing that one thousand families in this city would be constant customers for infants' flesh, beside others who might have it at merry-meetings, particularly at weddings and christenings, I compute that Dublin would take off annually about twenty thousand carcasses; and the rest of the kingdom (where probably they will be sold somewhat cheaper) the remaining eighty thousand.

I can think of no one objection, that will possibly be raised against this proposal, unless it should be urged, that the number of people will be thereby much lessened in the kingdom. This I freely own, and it was indeed one principal design in offering it to the world. I desire the reader will observe, that I calculate my remedy for this one individual kingdom of Ireland, and for no other that ever was, is, or I think ever can be, upon earth. Therefore let no man talk to me of other expedients: of taxing our absentees at five shillings a pound: of using neither clothes, nor household furniture, except what is our own growth and manufacture: of utterly rejecting the materials and instruments that promote foreign luxury: of curing the expensiveness of pride, vanity, idleness, and gaming in our women: of introducing a vein of parsimony, prudence and temperance: of learning to love our country, in the want of which we differ even from LAPLANDERS, and the inhabitants of TOPINAMBOO[21]: of quitting our animosities and factions, nor acting any longer like the Jews, who were murdering one another at the very moment their city was taken: of being a little cautious not to sell our country and conscience for nothing: of teaching landlords to have at least one degree of mercy toward their tenants: lastly, of putting a spirit of honesty, industry, and skill into our shopkeepers; who, if a resolution could now be taken to buy only our native goods, would immediately unite to cheat and exact upon[22] us in the price, the measure, and goodness, nor could ever yet be brought to make one fair proposal of just dealing, though often and earnestly invited to it.

Therefore I repeat, let no man talk to me of these and the like expedients, till he has at least some glimpse of hope, that there will be ever some hearty and sincere attempt to put them in practice.

But, as to myself, having been wearied out for many years with offering vain, idle, visionary thoughts, and at length utterly despairing of success, I fortunately fell upon this proposal; which, as it is wholly new, so it has something solid and real, of no expense and little trouble, full in our own power, and whereby we can incur no danger in disobliging ENGLAND. For this kind of commodity will not bear exportation, the flesh being of too tender a consistence to admit a long continuance in salt, although perhaps I could name a country[23], which would be glad to eat up our

---

21. Laplanders; (i.e.) even Laplanders love their frozen, infertile country and the savage tribes of Brazil their jungle more than the Anglo-Irish love Ireland.
22. 뒤집어 씌우다
23. England

whole nation without it.

After all, I am not so violently bent upon my own opinion as to reject any offer proposed by wise men, which shall be found equally innocent, cheap, easy, and effectual. But before something of that kind shall be advanced in contradiction to my scheme, and offering a better, I desire the author, or authors, will be pleased maturely to consider two points. First, as things now stand, how they will be able to find food and raiment for a hundred thousand useless mouths and backs. And, secondly, there being a round million of creatures in human figure throughout this kingdom, whose whole subsistence put into a common stock would leave them in debt two millions of pounds sterling, adding those who are beggars by profession, to the bulk of farmers, cottagers, and labourers, with the wives and children who are beggars in effect; I desire those politicians who dislike my overture[24], and may perhaps be so bold as to attempt an answer, that they will first ask the parents of these mortals, whether they would not at this day think it a great happiness to have been sold for food at a year old, in the manner I prescribe, and thereby have avoided such a perpetual scene of misfortunes, as they have since gone through, by the oppression of landlords, the impossibility of paying rent without money or trade, the want of common sustenance, with neither house nor clothes to cover them from the inclemencies of the weather, and the most inevitable prospect of entailing the like, or greater miseries, upon their breed for ever.

I profess, in the sincerity of my heart, that I have not the least personal interest in endeavouring to promote this necessary work, having no other motive than the public good of my country, by

24. proposal

advancing our trade, providing for infants, relieving the poor, and giving some pleasure to the rich. I have no children by which I can propose to get a single penny; the youngest being nine years old, and my wife past childbearing.

EXERCISES

A. *Answer the following questions.*

1. Does the essay shock you? Was it the author's purpose to shock you?
2. Do you think the author proposes a reasonable solution to the horrors of Irish poverty under English domination?
3. What specific Irish problems does the author state and what specific solutions does he propose?
4. What is the main target of his attack?
5. What is the dramatic irony of this essay?

B. *Fill in the blanks with suitable words.*

1. The children, all in rags, were importuning every passenger (　　) an alms.
2. Those infants, as they grow up, either turn thieves for want (　　) work, or leave their dear native country.
3. But my intention is very (　　) from being confined to provide only for the children of professed beggars.
4. They shall, (　　) the contrary, contribute to the feeding and partly to the clothing, of many thousands.
5. I shall now humbly propose my own thoughts, which I hope

will not be liable ( ) the least objection.

6. The flesh will be ( ) season throughout the year, but more plentifully in March.
7. A great number of both sexes in every country are now ready to starve for want ( ) work and service.
8. Some scrupulous people might be apt to censure such a practice as a little bordering ( ) cruelty.
9. Neither indeed can I deny, that, if the same use were ( ) of several plump young girls in this town, the kingdom would not be the worse.
10. They have chosen rather to leave their country than stay at home and pay tithes ( ) their conscience to an Episcopal curate.
11. I have no children ( ) which I can propose to get a single penny.
12. I have no other motive ( ) the public good of my country.

C. *Give the correct forms of the words given in the brackets.*

1. I am assured by our merchants, that a boy or a girl before twelve years old is no (sale) commodity.
2. I have been assured by a very (know) American of my acquaintance that a young healthy child is a most delicious and wholesome food.
3. When the family dines alone, the fore or hind quarter will make a (reason) dish.
4. If at any time they are (accident) hired to common labour, they have not strength to perform it.
5. As I have already observed, it would greatly (less) the number of Papists, with whom we are yearly over-run.
6. The poorer tenants will have something (value) of their own,

which may help to pay their landlord's rent.

7. The (maintain) of a hundred thousand children, from two years old and upwards, cannot be computed at less than ten shillings a piece.
8. And the money will circulate among ourselves, the goods (be) entirely of our own growth and manufacture.
9. They have their houses (frequent) by all the fine gentlemen.
10. This would be great (induce) to marriage, which all wise nations have either encouraged by rewards, or enforced by laws and penalties.
11. They are no way (compare) in taste or magnificence to a well-grown, fat, yearling child.
12. I profess, in the (sincere) of my heart, that I have not the least personal interest in endeavouring to promote this necessary work.

편저자 : 조 석 종
경기대학교 영어영문학과 교수 역임

ADVANCED ENGLISH READINGS

1판 1쇄 찍음 • 1996년 2월 22일
1판 4쇄 펴냄 • 2006년 8월 20일

편저자 • 조 석 종
발행인 • 정 현 걸
발 행 • 신 아 사
인 쇄 • 현대문화사

출판등록 • 1956년 1월 5일 (제9-52호)
서울특별시 은평구 녹번동 28-36번지 2F
전화 (02)382-6411 • 팩스 (02)382-6401
홈페이지 • www.shinasa.co.kr
이메일 • shinasa@chol.com

정가 ***10,000*** 원